Expert Driving the Police Way

Expert Driving the Police Way

John Miles

Diagrams by Ronald Morley
Photographs by Carl Bruin

PETER DAVIES : LONDON

(629.2)

47344

PRINTED IN GREAT BRITAIN BY
MORRISON AND GIBB LTD., LONDON AND EDINBURGH

Contents

Contents

Illustrations

The aims of this book are:

1. To save lives;
2. To make driving more enjoyable;
3. To make drivers safer at the high speeds of which nearly all cars today are capable.

JOHN MILES
London, 1970

1

Why Drive the Police Way?

A well-known boxer noted more for attack than defence was asked what he did after a big fight and he answered: 'Bleed'. He was only half joking, because this particular fighter never bothered to learn the basic skills for his dangerous job.

The moral for drivers is obvious. No sane motorist—and I am assuming that all motorists are sane, although some people may disagree—wants to become a bleeding heap in the gutter, surrounded by other bleeding heaps who are there because of him. So a sane motorist appreciates that car-driving can be safe or dangerous, and the difference depends mainly on the skill of the driver. I can illustrate how safety is increased by learning the skills of a good driving technique, especially the police technique which I know so well and taught for so long to men intended for the Flying Squad and other top units which required advanced training. The illustration is from Metropolitan Police history.

First Police Cars

London police chiefs have been aware of the importance of mobility since 1758, the year the Bow Street Runners were allowed to stop running and ride horses. About one hundred years later wheeled vehicles were added, including some remarkable chocolate-coloured hand ambulances which were used to cart the sick and the wounded, the dead and the dead drunk to hospitals, mortuaries or police stations. (Incredibly, the last of these remained officially in service until 1938.) In 1903 the Motor Car Act allowed vehicles propelled by the internal combustion engine to travel on highways without a man in front waving a red flag, and that same year the Metropolitan Police bought its first two motor-cars. They had the enviable numbers A209 and A210, numbers still associated with the police, although no longer on ancient, seven-and-a-half horse-power Wolseleys.

After the First World War the Met bought several ex-Royal Flying Corps Crossley tenders and in 1920 some of these became the first wireless cars, and the Flying Squad was formed. They were equipped with collapsible aerials which, when up, looked like giant bedsteads. During the twenties and early thirties the Squad used Lea Francis, M.G., Invicta, Bentley, Lagonda and Railton cars, and rather haphazard training was given at Lambeth Garage. In 1932 training and testing became more formal and drivers were graded A, B, or C. The A Class drove Flying Squad cars, the B drivers drove any other kind of car, and the C men could drive only specified makes of police car.

Early Police Driving

There is no reason to suppose that the police drivers of those days were any worse than the ordinary civilian drivers of today. The test they had to pass was at least as difficult as the present MoT test—in fact I am sure it was more difficult—but driving police cars is a demanding occupation and by 1934 the accident rate in the Metropolitan Police Area was one in every 8,000 miles. We used to joke that in those days there was not a stone left unturned between Scotland Yard and the Lambeth Garage, because every one had been hit by a police car. Yet the standard of driving was far from bad.

Sir Malcolm Campbell in 1934 gave severe tests to a large number of police drivers under different road conditions and at different speeds and was full of praise for their skill. Nevertheless the number of accidents had to be reduced, so in January, 1935, the first specialist police driving school was opened, and in 1937 the late Earl of Cottenham, a racing driver from Alvis and Sunbeam teams, was put in charge. He really started things moving, and by 1938 the accident rate had dropped to one in every 27,000 miles.

Effect of 'the System'

That achievement in just a bit more than one year is pretty sensational evidence of the way training and skill increase safety, but the accident figure for Metropolitan Police drivers today provides even more dramatic evidence. In 1938 the training facilities were not sufficient for the Cottenham technique to be taught thoroughly and mastered completely by every driver in the Force. That only became possible with time and improved facilities, and today's accident figure shows the final result.

Nowadays there is more traffic on the roads, more criminals are at work, more speeding cars have to be chased and at higher speeds than in 1938, yet the accident rate for the Met has dropped to one in every 70,000 miles. The general hazards of all driving and police driving in particular have increased a lot since 1934, yet police drivers are nine times safer purely as a result of learning how to use always a driving formula devised by Lord Cottenham. That is the only reason for the improvement. If police cars were driven by men who had done nothing more than pass their MoT tests the accident rate undoubtedly would be worse than in 1934 because of the extra traffic, extra speed and extra work, which shows the difference made by knowledge and training.

So what was the magic introduced by Lord Cottenham and his associates? Lord Cottenham produced a system for driving which, if adhered to, makes it impossible to have accidents. Police drivers do have accidents, as the figures show, but never when driving strictly by the book, and the book in question is *Roadcraft*, the police driving manual.

Use of *Roadcraft*

Members of the public can buy *Roadcraft* from H.M. Stationery Office, but I doubt if many obtain full value from it, because in the police *Roadcraft* is used in conjunction with a series of lectures which explain its exact meaning, and without these lectures and explanations parts can be misinterpreted with unfortunate results. I have met very few who, without practical help, were able to apply the whole of the principles of *Roadcraft* just by studying the book. There are various possible examples of this misinterpretation, but in my experience the most obvious is the cornering technique outlined in the book. Practically every person I have met who has read *Roadcraft* and not had it explained more fully has misunderstood the instructions for going round corners, with the result that they negotiate bends and corners in a bad and potentially dangerous manner. Yet when the *Roadcraft* cornering method is explained fully and understood correctly it is the safest and most sensible technique in the world.

Another problem with *Roadcraft* is that some important things are omitted completely: for example there is no section devoted to overtaking. The reason is that overtaking is regarded simply as approaching and coping with a hazard—just like a bend or roundabout—and the way in which the system for dealing with hazards applies to overtaking is covered in the lectures and by demonstration.

In this book I intend to explain these and all other driving manoeuvres completely, thoroughly and simply, as I did in my lectures to police students at Hendon, and will use diagrams and photographs to replace the practical demonstrations that were an important part of the teaching at Hendon.

I hope it does not sound presumptuous of me to assume that I can do this, but I know *Roadcraft* almost by heart and naturally I know every possible variation on the lectures which I gave for years to explain *Roadcraft* more fully. Besides that, I know which points caused trouble for hundreds of motoring students, I know the mistakes they made at the wheel, the reasons for the mistakes and the words I used to help correct them. (In practice, that included rude words, but I will leave them out of the book!)

The Way to be a Good Driver

At Hendon people often used to say to me and to the other instructors: 'I don't know how you do it.' Well, I will tell you how I personally did it. Bloody hard work coupled with the fact that in my youth I listened to my elders and betters. Learning to drive safely and well *is* hard work, but once you have learned you never forget. It takes three separate full-time courses lasting a total of twelve weeks to become a Class I police driver, and there must be thousands of miles of police driving between the courses. In my day only a Class I driver could apply to become an instructor, and those accepted were put on another course lasting six weeks. Those who came through the stiff test at the end became instructors and those who did not went back on cars; and a few lost their Class I certificates at the same time.

Throughout each course *Roadcraft* is the Bible and the

Highway Code the catechism. Every police driver must drive by *Roadcraft*, even if there are one or two minor points with which he disagrees. In effect each policeman is told: You are going to drive the Commissioner's car, or the Chief Constable's car, and you will drive it this way.

As long as the car is being driven that way it is impossible to have an accident. Police drivers are not allowed to have accidents. If a serious accident does occur the driver has to go before a board of inquiry, rather like the court martial of a captain who loses his ship, and he is asked to explain what happened. And at every inquiry somebody at some time is going to say to the unfortunate policeman: 'If you had been driving according to the book surely this could not have happened.'

The driver then has to explain why he was not driving by the book. Perhaps he was chasing a bandit car and took a calculated risk. If so he has to give a jolly good reason why the risk was necessary, and it makes no difference whether he is a Flying Squad driver chasing a train robber or a traffic patrol after a speeding Aston that can go 50 miles an hour faster than the police car. Accidents are not allowed under any circumstances, and cannot happen if the car is being driven correctly and in the proper police manner.

Origin of 'the System'

'The book' and the attitude to driving and accidents are a direct result of the work of Lord Cottenham, who made a pretty scientific study of driving and obviously discussed it with his racing colleagues before he produced his system. The basic principle sounds trite today, but it is still just as true as when Lord Cottenham first put it into words after he took over the Hendon school. Boiled down to its essentials that principle is that nothing can go wrong if your position, speed and gear are right.

I suppose there was nothing sensationally new in discovering this, because it applies to so many other things. People had been jumping horses long before there were motor-cars, and if they were in the wrong place at the wrong speed at the wrong time they probably went through whatever they were trying to jump, or else they went over and the horse did not. The same principle must apply to life itself. There are people who became millionaires simply because they were in the right place at the right time and able to move at the right speed.

However Lord Cottenham did more than just put the principle into words. He worked out driving plans and programmes to ensure that one always was in the right position, at the right speed and in the right gear, and passed on his theories to the first Hendon instructors who made copious notes. Later these notes were combined and duplicated and lent to students on the various courses, and it was these duplicated notes which eventually became the basis for *Roadcraft*.

Lord Cottenham and his disciplined system for driving have had more influence on motoring generally throughout the world than any other man or programme. His work originally was for the Metropolitan Police, but now *Roadcraft* is used by all British police forces. Besides that, selected Ministry driving examiners, ambulance drivers, Fire Brigade drivers and men from the Forces were trained at Hendon to assist each group in setting up a driving school based on the same training ideas.

Police drivers have come from nearly forty foreign countries, ranging from Aden to Iceland, from Syria to the Solomon Islands. The Royal Canadian Air Force sent men to learn the Hendon way. I assume that in each case the training has been adapted to local needs and now influences road behaviour in the country concerned.

Lord Cottenham may have been responsible for saving thousands of lives, and all because he was asked by the Met

Police to devise a method of driving police cars safely and quickly, and in such a way that there would be minimum damage to the cars and to the public.

His technique may one day save your life if you study and learn it properly. This book is to help you do that.

2

✦

The Driver

The skills needed to drive a motor-car properly cannot be split up into neat little compartments. Everything a driver does will affect the motoring situation around him. If he does one thing wrong it usually leads to other wrong things, or may be the result of other wrong things. If a man's overtaking is wrong, then his approach to the overtaking must have been wrong, and if his approach is wrong then his road observation must have been wrong. Too many people try to separate things and say 'You made a mistake here' when in fact the mistake started half a minute earlier or half a mile back.

Very often people blame gear-changing or braking or steering for a fault or series of faults when the real error is in the driver's mind and mental attitude. Many people start off with the wrong attitude and never learn the right one. The average learner goes to a driving school and buys a series of lessons just as he would buy a chair from Harrods or a loaf from the baker. He feels he has bought and paid for something which will be delivered to the door, and that's that. No more effort is needed. He will have his lessons and then pass his driving test and become a motorist entitled to go out and die at 100 m.p.h.

Learning the Wrong Way and Right Way

Some unqualified or amateur instructors do very little to help by saying that first you learn to pass the test and then you start learning to drive. This creates the wrong attitude in those learners who did not have the wrong attitude already. It also shows that the teacher himself has the wrong approach to the whole question of driving, and I would advise any learner who comes across such a person to take his lessons from a qualified instructor who has Ministry of Transport approval. A beginner should start learning to drive from the moment he gets into the car, and he should be learning to drive properly. A novice should drive in exactly the same way as an experienced and well-trained driver, except that he will be less adept and will take a little longer to do things, and therefore, I hope, will not attempt to drive so quickly. I consider that a learner who passes his MoT test is still a novice, because the test has simply shown that he knows how to manage the machine with some small degree of skill.

The Test

I am not saying that the MoT test is too easy. I do not go along with those people who say that we should have a harder test, because there can be no harder test than asking a man to get in and drive. It would be nice, however, to have a test that was more comprehensive, and covered more aspects of motoring. There was a series of dramatic advertisements on television comparing bad overtaking to Russian roulette, and a smoking revolver was featured. Towards the end of the advertisement a voice said: 'You know how to do it properly. . . .' In fact, that statement was rubbish. One has only to drive a long journey to see that few drivers really know how to overtake properly.

Without going into long discussions about the driving test, I question the wisdom of the Ministry in putting out advertisements telling motorists that they know how to overtake properly when it is patently obvious on the roads that many people do not, and when there does not exist any generally recognised system for teaching the public how to overtake. The wording in that advertisement could help to foster that dangerous I-know-it-all attitude which causes so much trouble on the roads.

I have had as much training in road driving as it is possible to obtain in this country, probably as much as can be obtained anywhere in the world, yet I am prepared to admit that I do not know it all. Every driving day one meets new situations, and no single driver can have met every combination of circumstances which may arise, so no single driver ever knows it all. There are people who think they know it all, and they always try to reduce driving to black and white. They say that you must always do this or you must never do that, and I think they are wrong. Driving is not all black and white, and people are dying on the roads because they have been told that it is. There is a lot of 'grey' that they know nothing about. Good driving is a matter of precision and should be approached with the open mind of a scientist, accepting that new knowledge may prove that some accepted rule is invalid. And one should realise that there may be an exception to every rule.

My own view is that I will drive by the methods I now use until somebody shows me a better way, and I accept the possibility that there may be a better way. Driving has been my hobby as well as my work for many years, and I have discussed every aspect of it with hundreds, probably thousands, of people, including students, other police drivers, driving instructors and racing and rally drivers, and for my own satisfaction I have tested things which they have suggested. So far, however, nobody has been able to improve on the basic techniques I was taught at the police school, and which I have since taught to others. Nevertheless there may be better ways, and I have always tried to impress this on students. The other fellow's point of view may be valid.

Fault of Defensive Driving

I do not agree with what is normally called defensive driving and the attitude of mind which it fosters. Defensive means that you must assume that the other driver will always do the wrong thing, which is the same as saying that every driver on the road except you is a fool. I agree that if the driver in front is going to do something, it is better to prepare for him doing the wrong thing than the right one, but that is not quite the same as assuming that he will always do the wrong thing. It is just part of your general preparedness for things going wrong.

Defensive driving creates the old cartoon situation of the mild little man who becomes a snarling monster behind the wheel of a car. It promotes the attitude that everybody else on the road is an idiot, and this, in turn, makes the driver believe that he himself is infallible.

The most important part of any motor-car is the man who drives it, and the most important part of the man is the brain, which directs all movements. A number of superb racing drivers have been physically handicapped, but they have overcome their handicaps by brain power which has given them the right mental attitude to driving.

Drivers Born to be Bad

Some people can never become good drivers. They can be made into better, safer drivers, but they can never become good. I remember at Hendon a bright young constable was sent to us because he was a good thief-taker and his superintendent wanted to put him into Crime cars. He was taught to drive, but he could never have been a Class I driver if he had stayed at Hendon for the rest of his life. He had no aptitude, and he had the wrong attitude because he was not really interested in driving and therefore could not concentrate. His mind wandered all over the place, and there is no room for that when driving fast cars, or even slow cars. It was not that he kept looking around for thieves, because a driver who is functioning properly will note everything around him as a matter of course. In a patrol car it is usually the driver and not the official observer who spots anything untoward, because a driver must be noting everything happening near his car, even things on the footpath and down side streets.

People who are uncertain in their approach to life rarely make good drivers. A man's character does not undergo a complete change when he climbs behind the wheel of a motor-car, and people who are generally uncertain tend to be what is normally regarded as accident-prone in cars. You know the sort. They seem to have accidents that were on their way to happen to somebody else.

There has been a lot of research into the characters of accident-prone people, and it has been found that many of them have the habit of changing jobs and/or wives rather often, while a high proportion have criminal records. People of this sort have a basic instability which is reflected in their driving and makes them reckless or thoughtless or just plain careless. (In proof of the exception to the rule, I have good reason to know that many people with long criminal records are magnificent drivers.)

Drivers Born to be Good

In my experience people who are good at ball games like rugby or football or cricket or water polo make good drivers, because they have judgement and rhythm. My ideal pupil would be a fit, fairly young man who plays rugby in the winter, cricket in the summer, perhaps chases girls a bit and probably has a drink occasionally. This sort of man sets about driving the same way he sets about everything, with enthusiasm and judgement and balance, and I would probably find it a pleasure to be in the car with him.

I have known quite a few young men like this as students at the Hendon school and sometimes I have found their driving suddenly go to pieces for no apparent reason, and when I have probed I have invariably discovered that there is trouble at home, or with a girl friend. That is enough to spoil their judgement, make them muff the occasional gear-change, or brake harshly too often, and it illustrates how mental attitude and condition affect behaviour behind the wheel of a motor-car.

Value of Experience

The reference to young men does not mean that I believe young men are the best drivers. Youngsters are alert and keen and dashing, but craftiness comes with age, and a crafty older driver will probably get there sooner than the youngster who is dashing about. There is so much traffic on the roads today that one spell of waiting in the wrong lane in town can waste all the time gained by hurrying along the main road. The older driver may not hurry so much, but he is less likely to be caught in the wrong lane, if he has learned from experience. Ideally one tries to impart to the young driver the wisdom that one has learned through years on the road—including, of course, quite a few hours in wrong lanes working out ways to prevent the same thing happening again.

Experience and a trained driving brain can make up for a lot of shortcomings in other directions. A man can have slow reactions and more than make up for it by developing good anticipation, so that he is never caught in a situation where lightning reactions are essential.

People with lightning reactions often rely on them too much, and need them in a big way because they keep getting into difficult situations through lack of planning. They are hard on their motor-cars and get into serious trouble if a mechanical fault develops suddenly. The worst examples of these people are most unpleasant to be with, as their driving is jerky and occasionally frightening. A good driver never frightens his passengers and never causes them to be thrown about in the seats, and he achieves this without becoming like those slow, boring drivers who are often so dangerous on the roads.

Slow and Frightening Drivers

A man has the right to drive slowly as long as he proceeds properly, carefully and legally, just as a man has the right to go quickly providing he observes the same rules. In my experience the man who drives fairly quickly is more likely to obey these rules than the one who crawls along. The more slowly people drive the more aimless and lazy their driving becomes, and the low speed limits on trunk roads seem to encourage this. A man who hurries along a bit keeps himself alert, and is more likely to enjoy his driving, as he should. His mind and his concentration will reach and remain at a peak. The man who always goes along at 40 or 45 m.p.h. thinks he is driving carefully and imagines nothing can happen to him or because of him, so he feels he is king of the road and allows his mind and body to sag. He will not make for others the allowances that the faster driver will make, because he feels that as long as he drives at his 40 or 45 m.p.h. all will be well with the world and everyone in it, especially him.

Very often the driver who travels at 40 m.p.h. or so on roads where 70 m.p.h. is permitted keeps up the same 40-odd through towns and villages where there may be a limit of 30 m.p.h., because he does not heed signs or think about what he is doing. In the days when I was on traffic patrol I did not pay so much attention to the drivers who were going smartly along an open road at a good pace. Most of them, in my experience, slowed down for towns and villages, and they were virtually all sufficiently alert and mirror-conscious to spot a police car behind. The slow drivers never seemed to know what was behind and did not slow down for towns, and these two things made them dangerous, in my opinion, and they deserved to be stopped for speeding. As in everything, of course, there were exceptions to the rule, and I often had to deal with nasty ignorant speed-merchants who did not care about anything else on the road, including pedestrians and children—and police cars behind them.

The Dangerous Slow Driver

I do not want to give the impression that I divide the world into slow and fast drivers. If I make any division it is between those whose outlook and attitude is wrong and those who have the right approach, and this usually is the difference between the bad drivers and the good ones. A man might, quite rightly, be driving slowly because he realises that he is a novice and needs more experience and advice before he goes faster. At Hendon we limited the novice students to 45 m.p.h. and the Class III ones were allowed to go up to 70 m.p.h. Classes I and II could go at whatever speed was safe for the conditions and the car, even if it meant that sometimes they travelled at 100 m.p.h. plus.

I have stressed mental attitude more than is normal because I believe it is the most important thing affecting a man's driving. A driver must have an attitude which encourages him to learn, to remain alert, to concentrate and to think.

Complete concentration is one of the most difficult things for a driver to acquire, and it will never be acquired by anyone who has the wrong mental attitude. One must be prepared initially to force oneself to concentrate. One must deliberately clear one's mind of all else and be extremely self-critical when concentration wavers for the smallest moment. Only by this sort of effort over many thousands of miles will one learn to concentrate completely and always when driving.

Fitness and Tests

Physical fitness is another important thing for good driving, although almost any physical handicap can be overcome, as I mentioned earlier, but it is essential to know that the handicap exists. A man could have slow reactions without realising it, so it is a good thing to have a reaction test on a machine, if possible. If there is no machine available one can try the old pound note game. Get someone to hold a pound note by one end, and have your finger and thumb parted level with the bottom end. The person holding the top releases the note without warning and you try to catch it between finger and thumb, and you are not allowed to make any downward movement chasing the banknote. Some with average reactions will only just catch the note. Some with the reactions of a racing driver will catch it after only an inch or so has passed downwards.

Another easy home test is for tunnel vision. Someone with tunnel vision has a restricted view of things happening to the side, and this may cause big blind spots when driving. Stand with your back to a wall and arms outstretched sideways with thumbs raised and knuckles touching the wall. Move both hands forward slowly until you can see both thumbs while looking straight ahead. A person with a full range of vision will be able to see his thumbs when they are only six inches or so from the wall, and anyone who has to move them farther forward has at least slight tunnel vision. Wing-mirrors properly adjusted are absolutely essential for a driver with tunnel vision.

Deafness can be a big handicap to driving, which some deaf people do not always appreciate if letters to the Press are any guide. I would suggest that they, too, have wing-mirrors and use them, and the car should be fitted with a tachometer to assist in changing gear without damaging the mechanism. However, I should say that many people afflicted in this way seem to develop a 'feel' for the vehicle which is not apparent in others.

3

<hr>

Check Before Driving

Once you are satisfied that you, the driver, are in good mental and physical order and fit to aim the motor-car in any chosen direction, it is essential to pay some attention to the vehicle itself, and there are some things which should be checked at least once every day. I am assuming that the tyres have enough tread and that the pressures are checked every week, either at a reliable garage or with a gauge of your own, and before every long journey; that the brakes are given adequate routine servicing; that the wipers and washers work correctly; and that all working parts affecting safety are tested regularly by your garage.

In addition to all this you should check daily that all lights are working. On most cars the dashboard tick and flashing light confirm that the direction signals work, but there is nothing built in to assure the driver that other lights function. If you have a garage you can make an easy morning check by fixing shiny tin-lids at strategic points so that they act like mirrors, and you can use these to check side and rear brake-lights. Failing this you can often tell even during daylight by the reflection in shop windows in town, if you bother to press the brake pedal and to turn on side lights.

Checking that lights work is easy, yet many drivers obviously do not bother, as one can see on the roads every night of the year. It is depressingly common for cars to be driven around with one or more lights out of action, including brake-lights. Any broken light can be dangerous, and two broken lights are four times as dangerous, especially if they are both tail lights and you are on a motorway. Another common thing is to see cars with the glass of their rear lights broken, so that those behind are faced by bright white lights, which become quite blinding if the driver happens to be braking and giving a direction signal as well.

Petrol, oil, water, battery and washer bottle should be checked every few days, but in my opinion a daily check is not necessary in a car you alone use every day for relatively short journeys. It is wise to check them all if the car is left unused for a week, because in that time you may forget just when you made your last check, or you may have a slow leak of oil from the sump, which can cost an engine if it is not spotted before you drive off.

Getting into the Car

Every driver should develop a fixed routine for checking things when he first gets into his car in the morning. The first check should be on his seating position, and there are many misconceptions about what is the correct position for good driving. If one is not sitting correctly one will not drive correctly and with full sensitivity, and this is so important that the check should be made daily.

One should lean forward a little when getting into a car so that one's bottom goes well into the back of the seat, because only then can one obtain full support from the seat. Next, check that your feet reach all the pedals comfortably, and by that I mean that they can be depressed fully without affecting your comfortable sitting position. Now you may check your arm position, and this should never be what is known as the 'straight arm' position with the hands holding the wheel at ten to two. This is one of the worst possible ways of holding the steering-wheel and it usually creates a bad sitting position as well.

There are times when you will need to have one of your hands at the top of the wheel (in the twelve o'clock position) during cornering, and if they are both straight in the ten-to-two position you will have to stretch forward when either one is at the top. This must involve leaning out of the seat, so that your only support will come from the wheel itself, which will interfere with your steering on corners and force you to grip the wheel so tightly that you will be less quick to receive skid messages passing to you through it.

The steering-wheel should be held lightly, with the hands anywhere between ten to two and twenty to four, and the arms should be bent. When turning sharp corners you should be able to move either hand from just past twelve o'clock right round to six o'clock, and this can be done without crossing your arms. People who shuffle the wheel through their hands a quarter of a turn at a time always steer inefficiently and usually do not have enough control on corners.

Good Driving Position

A good rule of thumb for finding a nice arm position is to adjust the place of the seat to a point where, with both shoulders against the back, you can hold the top of the wheel with straight arms. Then drop your hands to the points where you like to hold the wheel and you should be in a comfortable position with plenty of control.

The efficiency of straight-arm driving is a myth in anything but a racing car or ultra-special sports car with a small wheel in a truly vertical position. The idea that the hands must always be at ten to two is another myth, and this one arises from the early teaching at Hendon. In those days the cars used included things like the Riley one and a half and the Riley two and a half and the old sporty Alvis, and in all of them the driver virtually sat on the floor. The big steering-wheel was in his lap, and the only decent way to hold it was at ten to two. I have never considered this to be the only position, and improvements in design have made it possible and reasonable to hold the wheel lower down. I nearly always hold the wheel at a quarter to three, although in some cars I alter this because the particular design makes it uncomfortable.

People who use the straight-arm ten-to-two position usually sit with their bottoms far forward in the seat, practically on the end of the seat, and this means that they have very little support. I also think it must lead to spinal trouble. Perhaps this is where some of the 'slipped discs' come from.

After confirming that you have the right driving position a check should be made on the interior mirror. Sometimes I think I'm taller in the mornings than at night, because the mirror seems to be set too low. Obviously, what happens is that when I drive home after a day's work, tired and possibly a little limp, my spine is not as straight and stiff as in the morning, so at night the mirror is adjusted to a different position. Sometimes at night one may even adjust the seat to a different position, which is why driving position should be confirmed every morning.

Obviously one next checks that the gear lever is in neutral, that the hand-brake is on and that all warning lights and dials work when the engine is switched on and started. Only after all these checks is one ready to drive away. People who do not use garages should also ensure that every window is clear of overnight frost or dirt.

4

Balance

Balance is one of the important essentials for healthy, happy living. If the balancing mechanisms inside the ears are upset things go wrong and shift out of perspective. Constant disturbance to the little mechanisms can produce awful results, like seasickness and car-sickness and lots of other sicknesses. The same thing applies to a car: if the balance of that is disturbed the results can be even more awful, and if one is to understand how to drive a car properly one must first learn something about the things which upset or improve its balance. I will try not to become technical, because technical terms are for designers and the like, not for drivers.

The balance of the car is most important on corners, and there are forces and mechanical laws which influence the behaviour and balance at such times. Two results commonly referred to are understeer and oversteer, and there seems to be a lot of ignorance about what the words actually mean.

Understeer and Oversteer

The definitions of understeer and oversteer deal with slip angles, so I will first explain what these are, to make the definitions more digestible.

Slip angles are a result of the struggle between centrifugal

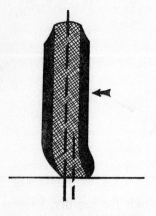

1. This is the shape a tyre assumes while cornering. Centrifugal force—the arrow—pushes the car and the wheel outwards, but the tyre tread which is in contact with the road surface resists the push and does not move outwards. Therefore the centre of the tread is no longer directly under the centre of the wheel, indicated by the vertical lines. The next piece of tread to come into contact with the road will be out of line with the tread now in contact with the road, and it will also be out of line with the wheel. This has an important effect on the behaviour of cars whilst cornering, as explained in this chapter.

force, which pushes a car outwards on corners, and the tyre adhesion which endeavours to prevent this happening. Centrifugal force pushes any turning object outwards, and the classic example of it in operation is a boy whirling a string with a weight on the end. Centrifugal force pushes the weight outwards as the boy whirls it. The same force makes a car move outwards as it goes round a corner.

The whole car and all four metal wheels move out, but the tyres do not because they are gripping firmly—one hopes—to the road surface. Since the wheel moves outwards and the tyre tread does not, the wheel is no longer directly over the tread. The elasticity of the rubber in the tyre allows the tread which is not actually or almost in contact with the road to remain in line with the wheel. The shape of the tyre, therefore, is distorted, and each new piece of tread comes into contact with the road slightly out of line with the piece before.

So when cornering there is a difference between where the wheel is pointing and where it is actually going, and the angle formed by this difference is called the slip angle. The slip angles of front and rear wheels are rarely, if ever, the same. If the slip angle of the front wheels is greater than the slip angle of the rear wheels the car understeers. If the slip angle of the rear wheels is greater than the slip angle of the front wheels the car oversteers. In practice, an understeering car tends to run wide on corners, and an oversteering car goes through a corner in a slightly tighter curve than an unsuspecting new driver might anticipate.

Effect of Tyre Pressures

There are some obvious things to be deduced from this and which affect the balance and behaviour of a motor-car on corners. The first is that, if tyres are soft and flexible, the slip angle will increase because extra flexibility permits a greater difference between the position of the tread on the road and the position of the wheel and the rest of the tyre above the road.

This knowledge can be used to make slight adjustments to the handling of a car. For example, the understeer of a car can be reduced by running with the rear tyres slightly softer than those at the front. Oversteer can be reduced by having softer tyres at the front, which is why some manufacturers of rear-engined cars recommend that the rear tyres should be twice as hard as those at the front.

Anyone who does decide to play around with tyre pressures to alter the handling of his car must take care not to exceed the tolerances permitted by the tyre manufacturer. The tread of a tyre which is grossly over-inflated takes on a circular shape, with the result that only the central part is in contact with the road. This makes it wear out quickly and unevenly, and there is also a bad effect on the car's handling and braking capabilities. If a tyre is grossly under-inflated the tread takes a concave shape so that only the outer edges are in full contact with the road, which again causes quick, uneven wear and upsets handling and braking.

Frankly, I think that to attempt to change the handling

E.D.—2

characteristics of a car by changing tyre pressures is something best left to experts. After all, most cars are a compromise, so if you cannot live with it perhaps it would be a good idea to buy another car altogether.

Centrifugal Force

The second thing to be deduced from the comments on slip angles is that understeer and oversteer are affected by all the things which affect centrifugal force. Slip angles increase as centrifugal force increases. Naturally a really strong thrust from centrifugal force pushes the car farther outward than a gentle thrust, so the metal of the wheels is farther out of line with the tread of the tyre, which increases the difference between the direction in which the wheel is pointing and that in which it is going. Thus a driver has to bear in mind the effect of centrifugal force on understeer and oversteer as well as its general effect on the adhesion of the tyres.

Centrifugal force is affected by three things—speed, angle and weight. The greater the speed when turning, the greater the centrifugal force pushing at the car. The sharper the angle of the turn, the greater the force trying to move the car outwards. And the heavier the vehicle moving round the corner, the stronger the force becomes.

This last point is one of the reasons why rear-engined cars usually oversteer and front-engined cars usually understeer. In rear-engined cars there is normally much more weight at the back, so centrifugal force is stronger there, causing a bigger slip angle. In a front-engined car the reverse applies: there is more weight at the front, so centrifugal force is greater there. This rule of thumb does not apply to all cars, but it does apply to most road cars that have not been specially prepared.

The effect of centrifugal force on understeer and oversteer raises a number of points to be considered. The first is that an

understeering car driven too hard round a bend will understeer so much that it will run dangerously wide; and turning
the steering wheel more sharply into the bend will make matters
worse because increasing the angle of the turn increases centrifugal force as well. An oversteering car driven too hard round
the same bend will have a marked tendency to spin.

It is easy to demonstrate these tendencies without danger.
Most cars on the road understeer, partly because of the front
engines and partly because they are designed to understeer as
understeering cars are more stable. If your car is one of these
pick a quiet road in which there is just enough room for a
U-turn. Check that there is no traffic coming and then make
a U-turn as slowly as possible, with full lock and the wheels
only just turning. Note how much clearance you have between
kerbs as you crawl round. Then make the same turn slightly
faster and note again how much—or little—clearance you
have. The difference will show how understeer increases with
speed, because the car will need several extra feet to make
the turn.

In an oversteering car the reverse applies, and I think it is
best to reverse the demonstration because it is more dramatic
to make the wider turn second. So if you have an oversteering
car pick a quiet road wide enough for a U-turn, make one at
your normal speed for such a manoeuvre and note the clearance. Then make the same turn as slowly as the car will travel
and note how little clearance there is this time.

Another point to consider is the way the balance and
behaviour of the car is affected by tyres which have been
allowed to go slightly flat, or which have been inflated carelessly. I will refer to the importance of tyre inflation in other
chapters when necessary, but the point that must be made
here is that you are going to be in trouble if you are driving
fast round a bend that you know in an understeering car that
you know when the front tyres are only half inflated. You may
also be in trouble if only one tyre is under-inflated.

Dangerous Mixture

Incidentally, it is this matter of slip angles which makes it dangerous to mix radial and cross-ply tyres. Radial tyres have soft sidewalls which permit greater slip angles. People have been killed by fitting radial tyres to the front wheels of understeering cars when there are cross-ply tyres at the back. So if you want radial tyres and cannot afford to buy five at once, take expert advice before buying any.

So far in reference to centrifugal force I have dealt only with its influence on understeer and oversteer, but of course it has another important effect on the balance and behaviour of a car when cornering. It can push so strongly that the tyres lose all adhesion and the car skids. Coupled with other forces, it can make a car overturn, and both these matters will be dealt with in later chapters.

Weight Distribution

The other thing which has to be balanced by the driver when cornering is the distribution of weight, which is influenced by braking and accelerating. Braking reduces the speed at which the wheels turn, but the body of the car keeps going forward at the previous speed until brought to a slightly jerky halt by the suspension linkages. This jerk, however slight, causes a definite weight transference from the back of the car to the front. If you watch a car braking you will notice that not only does the front dip but the back lifts, because weight is moved away from the rear end so that the back springs are able to extend upwards.

The reverse happens under acceleration. The wheels move first and the body catches up. Weight shifts from the front to the back, and you may notice sometimes that when a car is

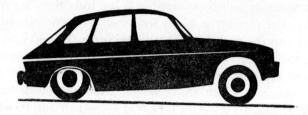

2A. Weight distribution changes during braking and acceleration. Weight moves towards the rear when a car is accelerated, and this can be seen by the way the back end goes down, the bonnet rises and things inside the car move backwards.

2B. Braking shifts weight forward. The bonnet dips, the back end rises and things inside the car, including passengers, tend to move forward. In each case there is a definite transfer of weight, and this has an important effect on a car while cornering.

being accelerated hard the bonnet rises and the back end dips down. This is only really noticeable in a powerful car, but it happens a little even in a low-powered car.

Say, for convenience, that the car weighs 1,000 kilos and the engine accounts for 200 of these kilos. So we can pretend that in a front-engined car the weight distribution is 600 kilos in the front half and 400 in the rear half. Under steady acceleration the distribution will be about 500–500, but under fierce braking it may be 800–200, which would be a bad distribution of weight for a car going round a corner.

Weight improves adhesion, and loss of weight reduces it. If

the situation described occurred in a car travelling fast round a corner the rear tyres might lose their grip completely and surrender to the push from centrifugal force. To make matters worse, the weight would not be shared equally between each wheel of the pair. A car being pushed by centrifugal force leans outwards, which shifts weight from the inside to the outside wheels. So if weight is shifted to the two outside wheels and simultaneously forward to the front wheels, the situation would be that possibly two-thirds of the entire weight of the car would be on the outside front wheel. So when the back wheels surrendered to centrifugal force the car would pivot on that offside front wheel.

Exactly the same thing happens whether the car is front-engined or rear-engined. Under braking the bulk of the weight shifts to the front, and under acceleration the load at the back is increased. So what do you do about it? Obviously you must go round corners and bends under drive—this will be dealt with completely in the appropriate chapter—but you must not accelerate too hard. There must be enough acceleration to balance the car, and not too much, because that can cause trouble. Experience is the only thing which will teach you how to gauge it correctly.

The sort of troubles caused by too much acceleration will be dealt with in other chapters too, especially the one on skidding. The sole intention of this chapter is to give information about the balance of a car under certain conditions, because one must know something about this if one is to understand completely the system of car-control devised by Lord Cottenham and explained in the next chapter.

5

The Basic System

The system of car-control is the foundation on which the whole technique of police driving is built. It is, quite simply, a formula for dealing with every hazard one may encounter on the road, and a driver who uses the system cannot be caught out by any kind of hazard, whether it be a roundabout, corner, bend, road up, another vehicle, a pedestrian on the road or even a boy on a bicycle. If the driver uses the system correctly in conjunction with the mechanical and other rules outlined elsewhere in this book, he cannot ever get into trouble.

The system, however, is not a magical jingle that can make every driver into a motoring superman. Two drivers applying the system to the same hazard are unlikely to travel in an absolutely identical manner, because one driver may have more natural skill and ability than the other. The system must be used by you to suit your own requirements and ability. When it refers to the right speed, it means your own individual right speed. References to the right gear mean the right gear for your particular speed in your particular car. The system will make you safe, but it will not overnight turn you into a Graham Hill or a Stirling Moss or a Jackie Stewart.

The system comes into use on the approach to any hazard, and it consists of a series of moves, all of which must be considered in sequence by the driver. Some may be omitted because of particular circumstances, and there are, in fact, some that

I think can be omitted almost all the time by ordinary road users.

The Hazards

In the whole of driving there are just three kinds of hazard. First there is the hazard caused by physical features ahead, and this includes corners, bends, roundabouts, hills and hump-backed bridges. Next there is the hazard created by other road-users, and this type includes slower vehicles which must be overtaken, broken-down cars which must be passed and tangles of traffic which must be dealt with. The third kind of hazard is created by things on or affecting the road surface, like pot-holes, patches of ice under trees, slippery leaves in autumn, mud left by lorries coming out of a field or building site or quarry, and temporary variations in the road surface itself due, perhaps, to frost damage or repairs or a lackadaisical local authority. A driver should go through the same mental drill on the approach to all of these, whether in town or on the open road.

The System in Full

In normal police teaching the system of car-control is divided conveniently into six parts as follows:

1. POSITION. Decide where the car should be positioned, and, if you have to alter course, check in your mirrors that it is possible to do so and give a deviation signal, if necessary, before you do it.
2. SPEED. Decide if you must reduce speed and, if so, check your mirrors again, give a slow-down signal if necessary and then start braking.

(handwritten margin notes: COURSE, MIRROR, SPEED, BRAKING)

EAR 3. GEAR. If it has been necessary to alter speed, change into the gear appropriate to your new speed.

4. SIGNALS. If a turn is going to be made, check mirrors again and signal if necessary.

5. HORN. Most drivers in Britain do not use their horns often enough when approaching hazards. At this point in any manoeuvre the horn should be considered and used if there is any possibility that another road-user (perhaps even unseen over a hump-backed bridge or hidden by trees at a cross-roads) may be unaware of your presence. Legally, of course, horns must not be sounded in built-up areas between 11.30 p.m. and 7 a.m., and in this situation one should use the headlight flasher

CELERATE instead.

6. ACCELERATION. Bear in mind the points between which you may skid.

can my safety be given away

I must stress again that these are all things which should be considered when approaching a hazard. In many cases the type of hazard makes a lot of them unnecessary.

Now let us examine the system in action.

Analysis of System

The system in its true and classic form assumes that hand signals will always be given, and in analysing it I will assume that the driver intends to use this form of signalling, although I realise that in practice hand signals are rare these days. I seldom use them because in most situations a mechanical signal is adequate.

It is best to assume for consideration that you are in a right-hand drive car on the left-hand side of the road and that the hazard is a right turn, because that manoeuvre requires more distinct actions than almost any other everyday piece of driving.

So, you are driving along correctly and ahead you see a

signpost indicating that the route you require goes to the right, and you must make a turn across oncoming traffic. The road has four lanes and you have to position your car in the offside lane, so you look in your mirrors to see when you can change lane without inconveniencing other drivers. You find you can move at once, although there is some traffic behind, which means that you have to give a signal to indicate your change of course. You give your hand signal and start to alter course afterwards, when both hands are back on the steering-wheel, because you can only have full control when both hands are on the wheel.

You must reduce speed to make your turn, so you check in your mirrors again and, if necessary, give a slowing-down signal to warn drivers behind that you are going to brake. You brake after the signal and with both hands back on the steering-wheel.

Once you have reached a suitable speed you will have to change into the gear suitable for the speed you have chosen. Then you check your mirrors again and give a right-turn signal. You now consider whether to use the horn, then you accelerate and make your turn in the way described in the chapter on cornering.

Everything has been done correctly in this example. You signalled your intentions well in advance, which is the correct thing to do. It is no good giving a signal which says, in effect: 'Look what I've just done.' Besides this, you had both hands where they belong—on the steering-wheel—each time you deviated from course and when you braked. And when you braked the car was travelling in a straight line. So, assuming your speed and gear were right, you have been perfect.

In practice anyone using the system completely would give trafficator signals as well as hand signals, and I think it would be very difficult to persuade the everyday motorist that he should give anything but trafficator signals. The system was planned for police use, and a policeman who is driving is working and has to obey the rules of his job, and if those rules say that he should open his window on a cold winter day and stick his arm out into the rain, then he has to do it if he wants to do his job, though the ordinary motorist is not likely to do the same even though the circumstances warrant it. In fact, I think the time will come when all cars are fitted with additional mechanical signals which will make hand signals completely unnecessary, but until that day arrives the hand signal has its place, in my opinion. There are times when it gives a better warning than any other signal, although those times are few and far between.

For example, on occasions a hand signal is the only way of indicating that you really are going to turn right and not just deviate from course. They are also valuable in crowded traffic conditions.

However, in most normal circumstances if you are turning right, I think it is reasonable to give just one trafficator signal before you change lane and to leave it on throughout the entire manoeuvre. On most occasions the slowing-down signal can be omitted, because brake lights are adequate. In any case, if someone is signalling that he is going to turn right drivers behind should expect him to slow down, so the prolonged trafficator signal gives prior notice that the brake lights will be coming on at any moment.

Hand signals, however, should be *considered* in case you find yourself in one of those rare situations where they help.

All braking and gear-changing should be done while the car is going in a straight line, as this helps to maintain the correct balance.

The System in Action

Now let us take another look at the system in action. You are driving along in the left-hand lane on a four-lane road about six feet from the kerb and want to turn right. You must change lane, so you look in your mirrors. There are two cars behind in your lane, and well away in the distance you can see three other cars in the right-hand lane. It is safe for you to change, so you give your trafficator signal, and after it starts functioning you move out. Now you check your mirrors again to make sure all is still well behind and start braking— and I mean braking, with the brakes—not changing down through the gears first.

The situation now is that the two cars directly behind noted your signal before you changed lane, and your braking reduces your speed sufficiently for them to go past in their lane. The three cars in the offside lane have also seen your signal and lane change and they also are able to pass on the inside and then move out to the offside again to overtake the two slower cars, and they have not been inconvenienced, nor have they been forced to reduce speed. The drivers of those cars, incidentally, should have been applying the system of car control to deal with you, the hazard ahead, even though you were far away.

Your next step is to change down, and you may start considering whether the horn is necessary. The fourth point in the system is signals and mirror again, but of course your trafficator is still flashing, so you just check your mirrors to make sure that no one has appeared at speed and is about to overtake you on the outside, despite your signal, your position and the fact that he will have to cross the centre line to do it. If all is clear behind and in front you start your turn and accelerate. Everyone should be happy and safe.

System at Traffic Lights

Now let us apply the system to a different hazard, a set of traffic lights on a busy road with three lanes in each direction.

You are in the centre lane some distance from the lights when they turn red, and three cars stop in the nearside lane and a lorry stops in your lane. You decide your ideal position would be in the offside lane, which has no vehicles in it ahead of you. So you check your mirrors.

Again there are two cars behind in the nearside lane and three more cars well away in the distance, one of them in the offside lane. You give a signal and move out to the offside, and when the car is straight again you cancel your signal and start braking. There is no need to give another signal, and you will not need your horn unless somebody ahead does something silly. If you are lucky the lights may change to green before you have to stop and you will be able to go straight on, if the junction is clear, in the offside lane. But you must change down to the appropriate gear to compensate for the loss of speed before passing the traffic just starting to move away from the lights.

The traffic moving away must be treated as another hazard, however. So you go through the system again. In the offside lane your position is right, so there is no need to alter direction or give a signal. The question of speed needs little attention either, because you are accelerating. As your speed increases you will need to go back to the higher gear. You may possibly need your horn if any of the drivers ahead acts thoughtlessly. Your checks in the mirror will by now have told you that the car which was a long way behind is closing and you will want to let it pass; so, as you pass the vehicles moving away from the lights, you will give a left-turn signal to show that you will move in from the fast lane soon. You do so when you are clear of the vehicles and then cancel your signal and accelerate on quite happily.

The system is applied to every situation in driving, including even a T-junction. Assume you are coming to a T-junction and want to turn left.

You are in the left-hand lane, so position does not need to

be altered, but you still check your mirrors and note that there is traffic behind to appreciate a signal. I think it probably is best to give your left-turn signal here, rather than later, so you give it and start to brake. The road across the top of the T is a major one, and your decision on speed must be that you have none: that you become stationary. So you brake to a standstill and then decide about your gear. If there is a lot of traffic on the major road you may choose neutral and change into first later, but if there is light traffic you will move into first. You are already giving your signal, so no decision is necessary on that and you will not need your horn. But you are going to make a turn and before doing so you must check your mirrors again, despite the fact that the cars behind are stationary like your own. There might be a boy on a bicycle or a girl on a scooter edging through and scraping the kerb, and he or she might be in a dangerous position when you start to turn. So you check just before you start moving and then you accelerate away to complete the manoeuvre.

You will notice from this example that I believe in early signalling. I can never understand the mentality of motorists who are waiting to turn right at red traffic lights and sit there without signalling. Signals are to help other drivers plan their next moves, and a car in the right-hand lane at lights with no signal flashing creates the impression that the driver intends to go straight on. The sort of driver who does this and gives a right-turn signal when the lights change will upset motorists behind and they may become angry; and an angry driver is a dangerous driver.

The One Fault

There is only one point which is generally misunderstood with regard to the system of car control as it is written. It stresses the use of mirrors when approaching any hazard, which may create the false impression that this is the only time that a driver needs to use them. In fact, a good driver looks in his mirrors on average once every eight seconds, so that he always knows what situations are developing behind. The frequent use of mirrors stressed on the approach to hazards is intended simply to confirm what the driver should have seen already.

But that is a minor criticism. In my opinion the system should be the basis on which every driver works to perfect his motoring and make it safe and enjoyable.

6

Moving off and
Gear-changing

Every driver should develop a fixed routine for getting into
his car and moving away from the kerb. Police teaching insists
on a routine, and most of us have developed our own little
additions to it. For instance, I always walk round the back of
my car and approach the driver's seat from the rear. It is easy
enough to see the front of the car from the offside door and
the driving seat, but you cannot see the rear properly from
either position. So I walk round and make sure nobody has
smashed the lights or let down my tyres or banged into my
boot. It also ensures that, if I have to reverse, I know there is
nothing lying low on the ground so that it would be invisible
from the driving seat.

The official police drill once again covers one or two things
that are not absolutely essential for the private motorist,
because a policeman may have to drive off in a car which was
parked by a colleague. In my own drill I include, as I have
said, things not included in the police drill, but both versions
have common objects. As many checks and adjustments as
possible should be made while the car is parked, so that the
driver will not be tempted to fiddle with things while in motion,
thereby allowing his attention to wander from the real job of
driving. Besides that, moving away should be done smoothly,

safely and without upsetting anyone else, including passengers and pedestrians.

Kerbside Checks

The first check on getting into the car should be that your door is securely closed, and if you have passengers you should do the same for the other doors. I am always amazed at the number of cars I see with doors improperly shut so that they could fly open with even gentle pressure. It is very dangerous.

Next you should adjust your windows to whatever position you think right. Then make sure the heater and de-mister controls are suitably adjusted. An experienced driver who knows his car can be fairly accurate with all these adjustments, but I think it is worth pointing out one or two things about windows and heaters. The number of cars with steamed-up windows shows that many drivers have never thought about or asked about the things heaters and de-misters and windows can achieve.

The normal heater system pulls in fresh air, filters it, warms it and blows it to the inside of the car. So it keeps increasing the volume of air in the car, and obviously if the air has no way of escaping the car interior will become pressurised, making driver and passengers drowsy; and they may even develop headaches. As the pressurisation increases the fan will find it more and more difficult to blow new warmed air inside, so the actual heating system will become less efficient.

If a window is opened even a fraction of an inch there will be no pressurisation, no drowsiness, no headaches, and the interior will actually be warmer because the heater will be able to continue at full efficiency. Another advantage is that the opened window—especially if it is a rear window—will cause air to move around the whole of the car interior. Since the air comes in at the front and escapes somewhere else, there must be constant movement, and this will help de-mist side and rear windows.

More cars now are being fitted with protected air-escape vents at the back, but even on these cars an open window may make a difference.

After heating and ventilation adjustments have been made, check that the hand brake is on firmly, that the gear lever is in neutral and that the driving mirrors are adjusted so that you can see in them clearly without moving your head. Then buckle on your seat belt and make sure it is fairly tight. A loosely fitting belt is virtually useless, because in a crash it allows the wearer to move forward several inches and then stops him with a jerk so that his head snaps down, with dire results.

All this detail for such a simple thing as getting into your motor-car may seem rather pedestrian, but the police method of turning ordinary drivers into expert drivers is based on having a routine drill for every situation so that it becomes automatic to do the right thing. I do not think that even experienced motorists can obtain full value from the police method unless I include the drills for very basic situations.

Moving Away

The most primary of all drills, of course, is the one for moving away from the kerb, and I hesitated before putting it into a book which is intended for people who have driven away from hundreds of kerbs quite successfully. Nevertheless, there is a right way and a wrong of doing even that, and I do not think any fault can be found with the police way, which means that it probably is the right way. Even on a level stretch of road the police believe in using the technique for moving away on hills.

The police drill is that you depress the clutch pedal for

about three seconds before moving the gear lever into first, then use your mirrors and signal that you are going to move out. Now you release the hand-brake catch but hold it in the 'on' position, accelerate gently and allow the clutch pedal to rise until the engine speed reduces to show there is slight loading. Move the hand-brake into the 'off' position and, as the car begins to move forward slowly, check mirrors again and look over your shoulder to make doubly sure that all is clear, let the clutch up more and accelerate more and turn the steering-wheel to move out from the kerb.

All movements from the first gentle pressure on the accelerator must be almost simultaneous. They must follow one another so swiftly that there is no time for any unusual wear on the clutch before letting the pedal up fully and moving the hand-brake to 'off'. I always start this way and I have never had a new clutch fitted to any car. My present one has covered more than 40,000 miles.

Kerbside Drill

The whole drill for moving away from the kerb in sequence is:

1. Ensure that doors are securely closed.
2. Adjust windows as desired.
3. Adjust heater and cold air controls if necessary and put on seat belt.
4. Check that hand-brake is on and gear lever in neutral.
5. Look in mirrors and start engine.
6. Give appropriate signal.
7. Depress clutch pedal for about three seconds.
8. Move into first gear.
9. Release hand-brake mechanism but hold 'on'.
10. Accelerate gently.
11. Allow clutch pedal to rise until clutch starts to bite.

12. Move hand-brake to 'off'.
13. Check mirrors again, and look over shoulder.
14. Accelerate and simultaneously allow clutch to come in fully.
15. Steer away from the kerb.

If you concentrate on doing all these things in the given order for a week or so the whole routine should become so automatic that you no longer need think about it, and that is what one is aiming for.

Why Gears?

Once you move away from the kerb the thing to consider is how and when and why you change gear. There are a lot of common mistakes in this, and if more people knew why, they would become more expert at the how and when. The simplest way to learn the basics of 'why' is to push a car for a while. You will notice that it takes a lot more effort to get it rolling than to keep it rolling, and more effort to increase speed than to maintain speed. The car engine has exactly the same trouble, but it is made easier by using the gears.

The gears are arranged and function so that in most cars the thrust applied to the driving wheels in first is about three or four times as powerful as the thrust applied in top. That is why it is so difficult to pull away in a high gear: there is just not enough power being applied to the driving wheels. It is also the reason why at a low speed you have more acceleration in a low gear than a high one.

Common Faults

If you are in a gear too high for your speed you lose acceleration and cause damage to a whole series of important and expensive mechanical parts. It is also damaging and inefficient to start off in second gear in a car designed to move away in first.

One of the most common faults in use of gears is that people do not change often enough. If you hear the engine labouring you should change down, in fact you should learn to know in advance when the engine is likely to strain and change down first.

Another common fault is in the actual movement of the gear lever. I have heard of learners who have gripped the lever so tightly that it has come right out by its 'roots'.

Moving the Lever

It is best to push the gear lever, with your hand cupped round it but not actually grasping it. Assuming that your car has the normal 'H' gate for the gears and first is at the top left, you move into that gear by putting your hand to the back right of the lever and pushing. Think of the gear lever knob as the face of a clock; then to go into first your hand will be positioned between four and five. Moving from first straight down to second your hand will press from about one o'clock, as this makes sure the lever does not wander across to the other side of the gate.

Going from second (bottom left) to third (top right) your palm should be placed between eight and nine o'clock, so that when the lever reaches the crossbar of the H it moves across naturally and up towards third. Going from third to top your palm would be around eleven o'clock, thus keeping the lever well to the right so that it cannot cross over to the wrong side. Try it a few times, and you will find that the positioning of the hand for changing down follows naturally.

By using this method of moving the gear lever you will never be damaging anything by tugging or forcing it. Pressure should be firm, but not fierce.

If I drive a car with a steering-column change I still do not grasp the lever. I push it, but I have found that it needs more practice to do it perfectly than with a centrally placed lever.

More Faults

Many drivers develop the habit of going along with one hand resting on the gear lever, and this is a bad habit. The ideal place for your hands while driving is on the steering-wheel, and they should be away from the wheel as seldom as possible and for the shortest possible time. Emergencies happen suddenly, otherwise they would not be emergencies, and in an emergency you need your hands on the steering-wheel.

Another common fault in gear-changing is that some drivers, especially inexperienced ones, keep the clutch pedal depressed for too long after the lever has been moved and allow the engine revs to die off, and this causes jerks which are bad for the transmission and make the passengers uncomfortable.

There are numerous other faults, most of which arise because the drivers have never learned or thought how a gear-box works. I think it helpful to understand the basic idea of gear-boxes and the part they play in making cars move.

Inside the Gearbox

There are three shafts involved, and all of them revolve. The crankshaft is part of the engine complex and revolves through the direct action of the engine. The mainshaft is part of the gearbox and is linked permanently but indirectly to the driving-wheels. If the driving-wheels are turning the mainshaft must revolve. When the driving-wheels are for the moment stationary and the mainshaft is then made to revolve, the driving-wheels are forced to turn. The third shaft is the layshaft, which revolves all the time the engine is running provided the clutch is engaged. It revolves through connection with the crankshaft and, by engaging a gear, transmits drive to the mainshaft and thus through the transmission to the driving-wheels.

The crankshaft and the layshaft are connected by the clutch. The clutch itself consists of two plates, one of which is joined to the crankshaft and spins when the engine is turning over. The other is joined to the layshaft, and when the two plates are brought together by releasing the clutch pedal, this plate and the layshaft itself must revolve if the engine is running.

The layshaft is fitted with a number of wheels with cogs, and these can be brought into contact—or are in contact—with cogs on the mainshaft. The cogged wheels are of different sizes. The smallest wheel on the layshaft connects with the largest one on the mainshaft.

The reason for this is obvious. If the layshaft wheel has fifteen cogs and the mainshaft wheel has forty-five cogs, then the layshaft will turn three times to make the mainshaft turn once. This makes it easier for the layshaft and its gear to make the mainshaft and its gears—and the driving-wheels—start turning. It is even easier if the layshaft revolves fifteen or twenty times to make the mainshaft revolve once.

Obviously if two gearwheels of different sizes are revolving at different speeds it can be difficult to bring them together properly without an almighty crash that is liable to rip the cogs off. Yet it must be done if you are to drive the car. On old-fashioned gearboxes without synchromesh it could only be done by skill. This is what happened:

Once the engine was started the crankshaft began revolving, and this, through the clutch, made the layshaft revolve. Once the clutch was depressed the layshaft began to slow, and after three or four seconds it stopped, all of which still happens. Once the layshaft stopped it was safe to move the gear lever and bring the smallest gearwheel on the layshaft into mesh with the largest wheel on the mainshaft, which is exactly what still happens on cars which do not have synchromesh on first gear. On occasions the gearwheels did not mesh together, and then the clutch had to be released and depressed again, which allowed the layshaft to revolve to a different position.

Once the car was rolling second gear had to be engaged, which meant depressing the clutch to disengage the crankshaft from the layshaft, but the layshaft continued turning. The driving-wheels were turning, so the mainshaft was turning and, as first gear was still engaged, the mainshaft was causing the layshaft to revolve. As soon as the gear lever was moved to neutral the layshaft began to slow down.

The second gearwheel on the layshaft now had to be meshed with the second largest wheel on the mainshaft, which was revolving. Obviously a stationary gearwheel on the layshaft coming into contact with the moving wheel on the mainshaft could cause trouble, so the layshaft had to be made to revolve and this was done by releasing the clutch while the gear lever was in neutral. Naturally the crankshaft made the layshaft revolve.

The clutch now had to be depressed again and the gear lever moved into second, bringing the gearwheels on the two revolving shafts into mesh. Then the clutch was released again. This process had to be repeated for each gear change upwards.

Double Declutching

Changing down raised a more difficult problem. Supposing you were in a gear which involved the layshaft revolving four times as fast as the mainshaft and you wanted to engage a lower gear in which the layshaft would have to revolve eight times as fast as the mainshaft. You cannot arrange it by the simple clutch work outlined above. You must do something extra to make the layshaft revolve that much faster.

The system was to depress the clutch pedal and move the gear lever into neutral and then release it again, as before. But now you had to accelerate, because the increase in engine revs would increase the speed at which the crankshaft revolved and this, in turn, would speed up the layshaft. Then you depressed the clutch again and moved the lever gently into the lower gear. That achieved, you released the clutch pedal.

This technique was essential for the old 'crash boxes' and is still essential for vehicles which do not have synchromesh on first when changes are made into first. The name for this gear-changing technique is double declutching, and it is always taught to police drivers.

Inside a Synchromesh Gearbox

A synchromesh gearbox works on the same basic principles, but the gearwheels of layshaft and mainshaft are always meshed with one another. They all turn at the same time, but the wheels on the mainshaft are not always connected to the shaft itself. Each wheel on the mainshaft can turn at a speed governed by the layshaft while the mainshaft turns at a different speed, and when you change gear you simply move a device which causes one of the gearwheels to be connected to the mainshaft so that they both turn at the same speed. The device slides along the mainshaft and becomes locked tightly to the next gear.

The device which moves along is a cone which slides over another cone protruding from the side of the gearwheel, rather like fitting one tumbler into another. The two cones, of course, are moving at different speeds when they come together, but their speeds synchronise as they fit together. Once the speeds synchronise, dog-teeth on one cone mesh with dog-teeth on the other and they lock together firmly.

This makes double declutching unnecessary, but if you change gear badly or too quickly you can damage the mechanism and make a noisy change.

Although double declutching is unnecessary with this type of gearbox you can get a smoother, faster change by double declutching if you do it skilfully. Accurate double declutching is good for the life expectancy of even a synchromesh box, but bad double declutching is harmful.

Heeling and Toeing

I invariably double declutch because that is what I was taught to do, and I have done it often enough on cars and police vans with crash gearboxes to know that I do it right. I also at times use the heel-and-toe method of changing gear, because in certain circumstances it is safer and more efficient than the usual method. Police teaching does not include heeling and toeing, which I feel is a mistake, because I think every driver should acquire every possible skill.

Heeling and toeing is used when changing down, and the technique can be learned fairly quickly. You brake with the ball of your right foot, depress the clutch pedal, move the gear lever into neutral and release the clutch pedal. Then you blip the accelerator with the heel or side of your right foot, depress the clutch pedal, change into the lower gear and release the clutch pedal. So you double declutch whilst braking.

On some cars the brake and accelerator pedals are placed so far apart that it is impossible to heel and toe, and if I owned such a car I would have the accelerator pedal cranked so that it was nearer to the brake.

You can see the advantage of heeling and toeing if you think about the system of car-control. The system allows a distance for braking and then there is a distance for changing gear, and in the normal way the two cannot be done simultaneously by police drivers, who always double declutch. The heel-and-toe method allows both manoeuvres to be completed correctly in the distance allowed for braking alone.

Double declutching down gives a much smoother change than the other method, and someone who uses the heel-and-toe technique can adapt it to give an almost unbelievably smooth transition from braking to accelerating, so it has a number of advantages if used correctly and thoughtfully.

Without the Clutch

There is an even more advanced technique, which I do not recommend any novice to try, and that is changing gear without using the clutch at all. The clutch is an aid to gear-changing, but if some other method is used to achieve the correct balance between the revs of the layshaft and those of the mainshaft perfect gear changes can be made.

Some of the finest gear changes I have ever known in my life were made by an inexperienced student at the Hendon driving school. We were out on a night drive and this student was making perfect changes, and I noticed that he also managed to dip the lights with every one, which was no mean feat considering that the car had a floor dip-switch to the left of the clutch. I thought to myself: 'That's clever.'

I watched what he was doing and realised that he was not even touching the clutch. He was going through all the motions of double declutching but using the dip-switch instead of the clutch pedal. But as he managed to get his revs right every time his gear changes were perfect. He was using an advanced and difficult technique without even realising it.

But please do not try it. You will probably make a lot of noise and damage something and get depressed. It is best to change gear by one of the following plans:

Double Declutching Upwards

1. PREPARATION. Position left foot over the clutch pedal and place hand on gear lever in appropriate position.
2. BEGINNING. Depress clutch pedal fully, release accelerator and move gear lever into neutral. The three movements are made simultaneously.
3. CLUTCH. Allow clutch pedal to lift completely, keep gear lever in neutral with engine idling.
4. NEXT GEAR. Depress clutch pedal completely and move lever into next gear, making movements simultaneously.
5. FINISHING. Let clutch pedal up firmly but gently and depress accelerator to make engine revs match car's road-speed.
6. LAST MOVEMENT. Remove foot from clutch pedal. Your foot must never be touching this pedal without cause, otherwise the clutch will wear out quickly.

Double Declutching Down

1. PREPARATION. Position left foot over clutch pedal and place hand on gear lever in appropriate position.
2. BEGINNING. Press clutch pedal down fully, release accelerator and move gear lever into neutral. The three movements are made simultaneously.
3. CLUTCH AND ACCELERATOR. Allow clutch pedal to rise fully, depress and release accelerator while gear remains in neutral.
4. NEXT GEAR. Depress clutch pedal completely and move gear lever into chosen gear, making both movements simultaneously.

5. FINISHING. Let clutch pedal up firmly but gently and accelerate.
6. LAST MOVEMENT. Remove foot from clutch pedal.

Changing Up using Synchromesh

1. PREPARATION. Position foot over clutch pedal and place hand on gear lever in appropriate position.
2. BEGINNING. Depress clutch pedal fully and move gear lever into neutral. Make both movements simultaneously.
3. NEXT GEAR. Move gear lever into next gear after fractionary pause in neutral.
4. FINISHING. Let clutch pedal up firmly but gently and depress accelerator to make engine revs match car's speed.
5. LAST MOVEMENT. Remove foot from clutch pedal.

Changing Down using Synchromesh

1. PREPARATION. Position foot over clutch pedal and place hand on gear lever in appropriate position.
2. BEGINNING. Depress clutch pedal fully and move gear lever into neutral. Make both movements simultaneously.
3. NEXT GEAR. Move gear lever into next gear after fractional pause in neutral.
4. FINISHING. Let clutch pedal up firmly but gently and depress accelerator.
5. LAST MOVEMENT. Remove foot from clutch pedal.

7

Reading the Road

The ability to read the road means, quite simply, that you have the ability to observe and to act correctly and intelligently on the things you see. If you cannot do this you cannot be a good driver. If you can do it well you will be able to anticipate trouble and avoid it, and you will be able to plan your driving moves well in advance, which will enable you to travel more quickly and more safely than other motorists.

A man in a slow car who can read well, plan well and think correctly will complete a long journey in less time, with less fatigue and with far less risk than a driver in a faster car who cannot read the road and plan accordingly. It is like playing a game of chess. If you can play chess only one move ahead you might as well give up, and if you can plan your driving only one move ahead you will drive badly.

The Right Picture

I have said earlier that the most important thing in a motor-car is the driver's brain, but the brain can only dictate the right action if it gets the right picture. So if you are missing some essential detail, or looking the wrong way on the approach to a hazard, the picture will be incomplete and your handling of the car must be faulty.

If a young man is driving and turns to gaze into the eyes of his pretty girl friend his brain will get the picture that all is very well indeed, yet the car might be tearing along the dotted line towards a head-on collision.

In fact, any girl who is out with a young man who takes his eyes off the road to gaze into hers should feel insulted. It means that he pays so little attention to her welfare that he is prepared to risk a crash which will throw her through the windscreen and cut her pretty face to pieces. And then there might be that awful but often seen kiss-mark on the bonnet made by the girl's lips as she hurtled to death or terrible injury.

The language of love in a motor-car is not the same as the language of love in a cosy restaurant. The boy who loves his girl—and the man who loves his wife and family—keeps his eyes on the road while he drives and does everything he can to keep her and himself safe from accident and injury.

Observation, of course, is only half the battle. Your brain must analyse and act upon what you see, otherwise you might as well not have seen it.

I had a pupil once who was pretty good as far as handling the actual car was concerned. He knew all about the mechanical side of driving and could balance a car nicely for corners and was good at skid-control. His driving commentary—when he had to tell everything he observed—was very good. He saw every road sign, he noticed everything he should notice well in advance.

But, having seen everything, he took no positive action at all until the last moment. He did absolutely nothing to avoid trouble which he saw building up ahead while he was well away from it. He would say in his commentary that there was a knot of vehicles ahead with slow lorries trying to overtake even slower ones and cars bunched up behind, but before he did anything about it we were right in there with them, when the sensible and safe thing would have been to hold back until they had all sorted themselves out. He would comment that there was a road sign saying slow, but he never thought it applied to him.

Classic Cases

One of the best examples of good reading of the road happened, actually, on a race track in 1950. The great Fangio was driving an Alfa Romeo in the Monaco Grand Prix, held on the narrow, twisty roads of Monte Carlo, and as he approached a tricky blind corner he noticed something odd about the crowd. The usual whitish blur was missing.

Fangio braked hard right up to the corner. He had reasoned instantly that if the whitish blur was missing then the crowd was looking away from him instead of at him, so they must all be looking at something which interested them more.

So Fangio braked and went round the corner slowly—and found a fantastic pile-up of racing cars on the track. If he had not gone round so slowly he would have crashed right into them.

More than half the cars in the race became involved in this one crash, but Fangio's ability to 'read the road' on a race track saved him, and he won the race.

I have never forgotten that Fangio story. There have been times when I have applied his reasoning at Monaco to things on British roads. For instance, if you see a few people standing staring at something around a corner you can guess there is trouble ahead.

There was another classic case with one of my colleagues at Hendon. He noticed two little boys dressed alike on opposite sides of the road, and braked. He guessed the boys were twins, and twins like to be together, so he thought one might run across to join the other. One did, without looking at the traffic, and he might have been killed but for the fact that my colleague was braking already.

Once I was out in Hertfordshire with three police students

and we came to a bus at a bus stop, and there were school children getting off. On the other side of the road, level with the front of the bus, I saw a woman looking across and leaning forward a bit and I guessed she was a mother meeting her child. I shouted to the student who was driving to brake hard and he did. We came to rest with the front of the car practically touching a little girl's satchel. She had been on the pavement, completely hidden by the bus, and she could not see us either, so she tried to dart across to her mother.

It was the mother who was at fault, really, because she should have had more sense than to be looking for her daughter from the wrong side of the road. But it was a good thing we were driving at a speed consistent with the conditions prevailing.

Effect of Speed on Vision

Speed plays an important part in road observation, because the field of vision narrows as speed increases. Ideally one should be able to observe things close to the car and things at a distance, but this is not possible if you are travelling fast. At 70 m.p.h. a driver's eyes are, or should be, focused as far ahead as possible, and this prevents him from noting things really close to his car.

I can illustrate this by citing the behaviour of pedestrians on a crowded footpath. If they are ambling along at a slow, steady pace all is well. But if one is trying to hurry he keeps looking ahead for gaps where the crowd is thinnest, and because of this he will keep bumping into people and shopping-baskets close to him. He is looking too far ahead to be able to observe things happening just a few inches away.

The same thing occurs when driving, which is one of the many reasons why it is dangerous to drive at high speeds on town roads full of cars travelling at the legal 30 m.p.h. If the speeding driver has his eyes focused on points far enough ahead

E.D.—3

to be right for his speed, he will not be able to note things happening close to his car. If he concentrates on events close to him he will miss important details farther ahead, with the result that his speed will be too fast for his effective range of vision.

Terrible Telephone Poles

There are many possible examples of everyday things which may be seen and will influence your driving. One that the police are fond of quoting is the old business of the telegraph poles. The advice is that you can gauge the severity of a bend by noting the line taken by the poles, and I think this is dangerous advice.

It will work perfectly ninety-nine times out of a hundred, but that hundredth time you could be in dead trouble. Sometimes telegraph poles take short cuts across fields while the road winds round a bend. At a place I know in Norfolk there is a very slight rise followed by a really tricky bend. A driver can see the poles from the other side of the rise and they go straight on, and any driver taught to rely on this sort of indication may easily be tempted to go over the rise too fast.

There are very few things which you see that will tell you that you are safe. Many things can warn you of possible danger.

Here are some examples to note when driving:

1. Fresh straw on a country road suggests that there may be a slow farm vehicle round the next bend, and who knows what sized attachment there may be on the back of it?

2. Fresh mud on the road warns you to expect some kind of building or road works or slow heavy vehicles ahead.

3. Passengers on the platform of a bus suggest that the bus will stop soon.

4. A parked ice-cream van warns you to expect small children, who may be hidden by the van.

5. Brake lights showing on a car at the brow of a hill suggest he may have seen trouble invisible to you.

6. Feet showing under a parked vehicle show there may be a pedestrian about to step into the road.

7. A county boundary sign warns that there may be a change in the road surface; or at night, that the street lighting may change.

8. A signpost warning of a school ahead means there will be lots of children about at certain times of the day; so check to see if one of those times is near. A 'children' sign means that they could be there at any time, so take even more care.

9. A puff of exhaust smoke from a parked vehicle shows that the engine has been started and the car may move out.

10. If you hear a factory siren watch out for thousands of people on foot, bicycle and in cars.

11. If you see cows ambling across a field towards the road, be warned that the farmer may have opened the gate; so there could be other cows on the road already.

12. A dog which moves its tail suddenly and is not on a leash may start running—perhaps across the road in front of you.

It is impossible to mention every point that drivers should look for, but the dozen above show the kind of thing which can be helpful. In police training we paid a lot of attention to driving commentaries, which indicated whether the driver was noting the right things and enough things, and taking the correct action.

I am including here a piece of commentary which I tape-recorded recently. It was recorded during ordinary mixed driving. I have not mentioned most of my gear changes because the main aim is to illustrate reading the road, but I do, of course, mention other mechanical things because they showed the action taken as a consequence of what I observed. So here is the extract:

Sample Commentary

'I am on the main road, which goes sharply downhill. I keep the car in third gear to hold it back. The road is rather narrow, two-way, and there is a vehicle parked on the nearside ahead. Mirror. Nothing very close behind me. I am staying out and coming closer to the parked van. The driver is not in it, so it won't move. Mirror. Lorry behind. Pass the van now. There are turnings left and right but I can see fairly clearly. There is a school sign, it's eleven o'clock and children shouldn't be about now. Mirror. Lorry is well back. Coming down towards the foot of the hill. I keep in third gear. There's a major turning on the left. Mirror. Lorry behind me has dropped farther back. Car in the turning waiting. Now going up the hill keeping a steady 30. Change of road surface ahead but new one's just as good. The day is clear, sun shining and there's a lorry moving off ahead of me. Mirror. The lorry behind is still as far back as he was.

'Road bends slightly to the right. Easing down, going round smoothly. Lorry ahead of me is going to the left. Mirror. No need for a signal. I ease out a bit and I can see clearly past him. There are two coming down the hill. Accelerate past him now. Mirror. He is turning to the left now. The road widens and then gets narrower. The road surface has been patched and there are all sorts of pieces all over the place, but there's plenty of grip for braking. There's a motor-cyclist overtaking coming towards me, crowding me for room, move left as far as I can. There are two very small children walking alone on the left, so I'll move out a bit and give them plenty of clearance. Mirror clear and no signal. It gives me a good view into the left-hand bend as well. Easing the pace down to about 20 now as the lorry ahead of me has his brake lights on. Nobody behind me.

'Traffic lights ahead are red. Mirror clear. Gently braking. Stopping now. Handbrake on and into neutral. Good opportunity to check my instruments. Plenty of petrol, oil-pressure is well up, temperature is O.K., dynamo is charging. The lorry behind has caught up and is stopping behind me. The lights are still red, plenty of traffic crossing. The road ahead gets even narrower, busy shopping centre. There's a blue van stopped on the left almost blocking the way. Lights have changed and move off very gradually.

'The lorry ahead of me will have trouble getting through past the blue van, and so will the one following me. It is almost single alternative traffic here. There's one coming towards me, but whether he has seen the blockage . . ? Yes, he has.

'The lorry ahead has gone through now. There's a cyclist moving out from the kerb in front. Mirror. The lorry behind is a reasonable distance away. I can slip past the cyclist, but the traffic ahead is stopping at a pedestrian crossing. Mirror. The lorry's still a decent distance behind and he's driving very steadily. Braking a little. The crossing's clear now. Accelerate a little now. Traffic ahead's slowing for a vehicle having trouble turning left. Now it's clear.

'There's a turning on the left and a blind one over on the right, but it's clear. The sun's shining down it and I'd see a shadow if there was somebody there.

'A very small roundabout ahead. Mirror. The lorry behind has dropped back a bit. I'm going straight on at the roundabout, so I slow down. I've got to give way, so slowing right down into first gear. I can go now. Into the roundabout and indicator left to show I'm going out at next exit. Pedestrian crossing's clear, and ground again goes sharply downhill. Make sure indicator's cancelled. There's a "steep hill" sign—one in ten. Keeping in third gear and running gently down the hill. The lorry behind has dropped well back. The road's falling fairly sharply away now and there's a black spot sign. Pedestrian crossing at the foot of the hill, and obviously that's the black spot. There are turnings left and right but I can see well into all of them. The pedestrian crossing is clear.

'It's a rather wide suburban road now and the surface is still patchy. Pedestrian crossing ahead and some people near it. I wonder if they're going to cross. They're hidden by a vehicle parked almost on the dotted line. Ease down until I can see. Yes, there's an old chap just going to cross. Mirror. Brake lights on early for the lorry still behind. Clear now, and I can accelerate away.

'Another parked vehicle on the bend ahead. Driver in it. Horn. I'll give him a warning. Numerous parked vehicles going round the bend and I am keeping well out clear of them. No need for signals. Traffic lights ahead are green. Mirror. Nothing behind to worry about; easing speed; they've been green for some time. They're still green, so accelerate over.

'The road's fairly narrow, good surface. Parked cars on the left and the driver ahead is signalling he's going to move out. Why leave it so late? If he doesn't come out he's going to hit them. His offside rear tyre could do with some air in it too. Quite a busy little shopping centre ahead. Big garage on the right and three cars in front waiting to turn into it. Mirror. Plenty of traffic behind but all going at the same easy pace. Fellow in front's going into the garage too. No signal this time when he needs it. Maybe he'll get some air in that tyre. Mirror. Easing down a little to pass the four cars in the middle on the inside.

'Plenty of parked vehicles on the left. Some pedestrians poking their heads through, looking at me, trying to cross. A walk of 20 yards and they could have used the pedestrian crossing. Nobody at the crossing. Traffic behind has fallen back a bit. All clear ahead and past the shops now. Road surface changes, very good. Mirror. There's a sports car coming up behind a bit fast. I'm doing 30 and he must be well over 40. Road goes right and there's adverse camber, but nothing to worry about. Easy bend, the speed's relatively low and road surface is good and dry. It goes downhill and the sports car isn't showing any signs of wanting to go by. The road bears to the right again and there's a railway bridge with a really sharp-looking left turn underneath it. Mirror. Sports car still comfortably behind, braking down now. Keeping out so that I can see, turning well into the corner so I don't go over the white line. Just as well I didn't go over the line because the chap coming the other way did.

'The road opens out now, three-lane. No footpaths—well, there's a bit of one on the offside but hardly worth talking about. The trees come right to the edge of the road on the left, so I'm keeping out a bit. The sun is shining through them and the shadows could easily hide somebody. Mirror clear. Speed limit now 40. Gently winding road, road surface good. Increase to 40. Another school sign. Funny to increase the limit just there! Police car parked in turning to the right over there. I'm doing steady 40. Sports car is turning right.

'There's a junction, major crossroads, ahead and I shall turn right. Road surface changes, just as good. I shall want to move over to the right in a moment. Mirror clear. Signal right, change lane. Mirror. White car behind now going right as well. Braking right down to second gear. Traffic coming the other way. After this one I can go. Mirror. I'm turning now. Up through the gears. Speed limit up to 50. Road surface good. Mirror, white car had to wait. Going up to 50 now. Road surface changes well ahead. Three-lane road. Mirror. White car well behind. Road goes slightly left and, looking across, there's a blue car holding the middle. I'm doing 50 so I can't very well overtake. Dual carriageway ahead.

'Mirror. White car well back. Chap in front seems to be slowing down a bit. Mirror. Red car coming up rapidly on outside, other cars have dropped back. Dual carriageway now, but still 50, nothing I can overtake. Red car passes me. Keeping to the left out of his way because he's stupid. He must be doing 80; if he breaks the speed limit by that much he's probably got no sense at all. He was nearly in trouble there at the end of the bit of dual carriageway. Idiot!

'The road becomes three-lane again now and there's a roundabout ahead. Mirror. Nothing behind to worry about at all. The roundabout has large "Reduce Speed" sign and five exits. I'm going straight on, which is the third exit. Mirror. There's a small van well back behind me now. Braking, second gear. Into the roundabout. Pass one on the left, second on the left, give left-turn signal to show I'm leaving by the next one. Out of the roundabout on offside and overtaking lorry which is very slow-moving. It's clear ahead now. Mirror. All right behind. Now there's a car and a slow lorry ahead. The car's moving out to overtake the lorry. Position's right, gear's right, speed's right. Going to overtake the lorry now. No need to use the horn. He's very steady, and now I'm past him and the car and back to nearside.

'Dual carriageway ahead. Mirror. Nothing to worry about. Into dual carriageway in offside lane to pass two lorries on nearside. Dual carriageway is two-lane each way here, but becomes three. Speed up to 70 and accelerating now. Road surface is very good. Now I'm up to 70. Mirror. Nothing behind to worry me. I'm in the middle lane and there are one or two lorries in nearside lane ahead and pile of cars catching them up. Mirror. Nothing. I'll move into overtaking lane early while I have plenty of time. In the overtaking lane at steady 70. Two cars overtaking the lorries now, so it's just as well I moved out. They're past one now, catching up on two. Second car is gaining a little on the one in front, so I'll just ease off a little. Flash my lights. He's steady now, so I'll overtake. Accelerate back to 70 and past one, two, three and clear and I'll move into centre lane.

'Road surface still good, road still three-lane each way. Nothing in front. Mirror. All right behind. There's a bridge ahead over the road, it's narrow and shouldn't present any trouble from crosswinds. Now there's parking 200 yards, but it's got a run-in lane and a run out, so that's no problem.'

8

Overtaking

There is nothing in motoring which has received so much official neglect as the art of overtaking. It has scant attention in the driving test, which as a general rule cannot include motoring on trunk roads; overtaking is one of the most potentially dangerous manoeuvres anyone can attempt in a motor-car, because it involves anticipation, judgement of speed and distance, the use of mirrors, positioning, gears, accelerator, steering, and two changes of course. It is not made any safer by the fact that at least one other vehicle must be involved.

As I have mentioned elsewhere, *Roadcraft* does not deal specifically with overtaking, because the proper application of the system of car-control will enable the driver to deal with any hazard. This particular kind of hazard is explained in detail by instructors in their lectures.

The official attitude seems to be that one does not *have* to overtake, which is strictly correct. Overtaking is a voluntary manoeuvre, unlike cornering, or going past parked vehicles. I suppose that theoretically a driver could go through his entire motoring life without ever overtaking at all, but I cannot imagine it happening in practice.

Time Exposed to Danger

Everyone recognises the dangers of overtaking, because it is a manoeuvre that on most British roads means driving for a while either on the wrong side of the road or in the so-called 'suicide lane' in the middle. Car designers refer to it simply as the T.E.D., and those initials stand for the ominous phrase 'Time Exposed to Danger'. Designers try to reduce the T.E.D. by creating cars which steer accurately and accelerate quickly from one speed to another with the minimum amount of gear-changing.

Every part of the system of car-control will probably have to be used when overtaking, and the driver must also know the effect of gear-changing and be able to make use of everything that can be learned in the chapter on reading the road. Besides all this a driver must develop acceleration sense if he is going to overtake smoothly and properly.

Now that I have said all that, I must also state that overtaking is quite safe and perfectly simple provided you know what you have to do and go about it carefully and properly.

The Principles

There are just two kinds of overtaking situations. There is the one where you have to wait behind the vehicle or vehicles to be overtaken until all the circumstances are right, and the one where you can see well in advance that the circumstances are right and will remain right, so you can overtake without any delay.

In each case the same three principles must be observed. Firstly, you must be able to see clearly and you must be certain that everyone involved can see you. Secondly, you must make certain that the other drivers—the ones behind, the ones ahead and the ones coming towards you—know what you intend to do *before you start to do it*. Thirdly, before attempting to go past you must be certain that there is a gap on the left for you to go into should you need to do so.

Unless these conditions are fulfilled any attempt at overtaking will be dangerous. It is not enough just to be satisfied that the road is clear, which is why I referred earlier to all the circumstances being right. One must bear in mind the other drivers, even the drivers one cannot see (and who may not be there at all). For example, if there is any sort of junction ahead the circumstances are not right, because there may be a car there, or nearly there, and there is a chance that the driver will either run straight into the road or allow his bonnet to stick well out, causing vehicles on your road to swerve.

It is because of the possible existence of these unseen drivers that one must *never* overtake in any of the following situations:

1. At or on the approach to a corner or bend.
2. At or approaching the brow of a hill.
3. At or approaching a hump-backed bridge.
4. At or near a crossroads.
5. Opposite to a road junction on either side of the road.

Other times when it is wrong to overtake for other reasons are:

1. Near a pedestrian crossing.
2. Near horses, except very slowly and quietly.
3. Where the road narrows.
4. Where you would force another vehicle to swerve or reduce speed.
5. On the approach to a school.
6. When you are being overtaken.
7. At any time when you do not have a clear view ahead.
8. When the driver ahead has signalled his intention to turn right or overtake.
9. When you are not certain there is a gap to move into after you have overtaken.
10. Where you are forbidden to cross the centre lines and would have to do so to overtake.

Acceleration Sense

Usually one has to wait for all these conditions to be fulfilled, and this is where acceleration sense is involved. Acceleration sense is, quite simply, the ability to adjust your speed accurately by using the accelerator without having to resort to excessive use of the brakes or to gear-changing.

Many people forget that the accelerator is a decelerator as well. If you lift your foot off the pedal the car begins to slow down, and a driver should be able to use this to reach the correct speed when he comes up behind traffic on the open road and is going to have to wait to overtake. It leads to smoother, more comfortable driving. Braking in such circumstances can be jerky and wasteful.

You should also be able to adjust the speed of your car exactly to the speed of the car in front so that you maintain your distance correctly without having to make constant alterations.

The Right Distance Behind

The distance which you allow between your own car and the one in front is a critical part of overtaking, and there are some misconceptions about what that distance should be. That is because there is a following distance and an overtaking distance, and there is quite a difference between the two.

The following distance is used when you do not intend to overtake and are simply part of a line of traffic, so that your main concerns are ensuring that you have room to stop or manoeuvre if necessary, and allowing space for faster over-taking vehicles to move into. A useful rule-of-thumb for gauging the following distance is to allow 30 feet for 30 m.p.h. and one extra *yard* for every extra mile per hour. So at 50 m.p.h. the

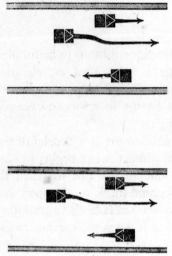

3. The diagram above shows a popular but wrong method of overtaking. The vehicle behind goes too close to the one in front before moving out, and then does so too sharply. The diagram below shows the correct method. The car moves into position gradually and is already going straight again well before reaching the vehicle to be overtaken. This allows the overtaking driver time to reconsider while there is still a gap to move into on the left and it shows other drivers the amount of room needed by the overtaking vehicle.

distance would be 30 feet plus 20 yards, making a total of 90 feet, which is roughly the length of three buses.

This distance allows you room to manoeuvre and enables you to see well ahead, so that you should be able to anticipate most of the actions of the driver in front. But it is not necessarily a good distance from which to start overtaking. Overtaking is like the classic recipe for jugged hare which starts: 'First catch your hare'.

The overtaking distance is usually shorter than the following distance and depends on the distance needed to maintain a good view ahead, the type of vehicle being driven and the traffic conditions. The first of these three is the most important.

The View Ahead

There is absolutely no point in following a furniture van so closely and so squarely that you see nothing but his back door and a bit of hedge on either side. If you do this you cannot see what is coming towards you, and oncoming traffic cannot see you either. Attempting to overtake from this position breaks every rule and is dangerous, even if you are driving the most powerful motor-car in the world.

In this situation you must drop back to improve your view ahead. If you allow the correct distance between you and the van, you will find that you can go a little closer to the crown of the road in safety and gain an even better view to the offside, and oncoming traffic will see you clearly.

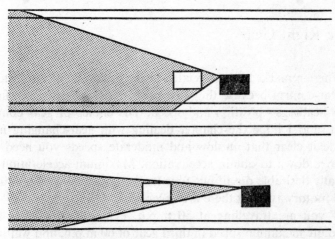

4. Forward vision is restricted dangerously by following too close to the vehicle in front. In the top drawing the driver can see very little of what is happening on the other side of the road and practically nothing of things on the nearside. The lower drawing indicates the improvement in vision obtained by dropping back a little. In this position it is possible to go closer to the crown of the road in safety.

This is where many drivers go wrong. They either lie so close that they cannot see whether or not it is safe to go, or so far back and are so slow in preparation that they only reach the vehicle to be overtaken when the opportunity to pass is lost. Then they have to start the process over again.

Acceleration and Traffic

The power of the car is important because of the differences
in acceleration. An ordinary family car may take between 13
and 15 seconds to accelerate from 40 to 60 m.p.h. whereas a
really powerful one will achieve the same thing in three or four
seconds.

The traffic situation is important because, if it is not flowing
freely, you may be forced to take up a following position until
it improves and then move up to the correct overtaking distance.

The Right Gear

These remarks have all related to the beginning of the system
of car-control because they deal with things affecting the first
two headings—position and speed. The choice of gear comes
next, and I hope the chapter dealing with gear-changing has
made it clear that at slow and moderate speeds you need to
change down to obtain acceleration. Maximum acceleration is
usually desirable on all but four-lane roads, dual carriageways
and motorways, but there are exceptions.

If you are travelling at 50 m.p.h. in a car which has an
absolute maximum speed in third gear of 60 m.p.h. and waiting
to overtake, it may be better not to change down. Third gear
may give maximum acceleration at 50 m.p.h., but you will run
out of punch as you near 60 m.p.h. and you may then have to
change gear in the middle of the manoeuvre. That would be
inadvisable, firstly because you will have to remove one hand
from the steering wheel at a critical time, and secondly because
the couple of seconds needed to change gear will rob you of the
advantage you acquired by changing down in the first place.

So the consideration of gear applies, once again, to your
speed and your car. A downward change before overtaking is

not something which should be done automatically. In the illustration I have just given the change down would simply speed you into the danger zone, and the change up would delay you there.

The System for Overtaking

I have made the point earlier in the book that all matters in driving are related to one another, and the overtaking situation where you must wait behind slower traffic is a good example of this. It also shows, in my opinion, how foolish it was to omit a full section on overtaking from *Roadcraft* when it was put on public sale. The system of car-control applies to overtaking as to every other hazard, but I think the manual should have noted the fact that in this situation it applies not once but twice.

There are two distinct hazards when you have to wait behind vehicles you wish to overtake. You must apply the system to make sure that your position, speed and gear are right for coping with the slower traffic ahead—your first hazard—otherwise you are going to hit somebody's back end. Then you have to apply the system again to go past, and the actual overtaking is the second hazard. But in the first application of the system you bear in mind that you wish to overtake eventually, and this will influence your choice of position and gear. If you do not relate the two uses of the system in this way your overtaking will be bad and time-wasting.

Once you are behind the slower traffic you start to apply the system again from the beginning.

Overtaking Position

The first point again is position and, of course, mirrors and signals. You are already in the 'waiting position', so your next position will be the one that will take you past the vehicle in front. Some drivers pass with a wide-swooping line, others crowd the vehicle on their left. Neither of these positions is safe, or desirable. In a three-lane road your desired position is in the middle. In a two-lane road it is in the middle of the offside half of the road. It is dangerous to occupy anything but these bold positions, although many people find this so strange that they are shocked at first. Just examine the problem, and you will see that I am quite correct in my advice.

It is always advisable for safety to leave at least four or five feet of clearance between your car and the vehicle being overtaken, even on a fairly narrow road. This may put you right over to the offside on such a road, but what is the difference? If the road is genuinely wide enough for only two cars, a third one coming in the opposite direction is not going to be able to squeeze through. So there is no point in going dangerously near to the one you are overtaking.

In a three-lane road a fourth car is not going to be able to slide through, so the same applies. If you occupy the middle of the centre lane you should have plenty of clearance on both sides.

(On roads out of town that are just too narrow for three lanes but plenty wide enough for two, some drivers have the habit of travelling dangerously close to the nearside of the road to allow another driver to overtake. This is most unwise. If the oncoming driver varies his position at all, the natural instinct of the driver in the centre will be to steer to the left. This must put the nearside car in jeopardy as he will have no manoeuvring room left to him.)

Point of Acceleration

If your mirrors tell you it is safe, you signal and move out into the desired position. You do not start accelerating before

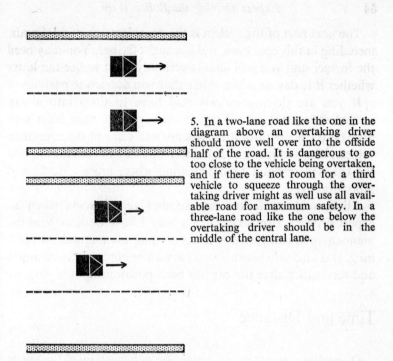

5. In a two-lane road like the one in the diagram above an overtaking driver should move well over into the offside half of the road. It is dangerous to go too close to the vehicle being overtaken, and if there is not room for a third vehicle to squeeze through the overtaking driver might as well use all available road for maximum safety. In a three-lane road like the one below the overtaking driver should be in the middle of the central lane.

you move out, because acceleration drives the car straight on and this increases any in-built tendency to understeer, pushing you closer to the car in front and making it more difficult to reach your chosen position. Beside this, it is a good thing to occupy the amount of road you need before you actually begin to accelerate past the car ahead. Other vehicles, including the one to be overtaken, can see how much room you want, and you yourself can make a lightning reassessment of the situation ahead while you still have a clear nearside to move back into if you so desire.

Once you are in position you consider speed and gear. Speed must be increased, and you may already be in the correct gear as a result of anticipating what was about to be required while applying the system earlier. If not, change gear now.

The next part of the system is the consideration of all signals, including in this case horn and headlight flasher. You may need the former and you will almost certainly want to use the latter whether it is day or night. After that you accelerate past.

If you are driving quickly and have to drop into a gap immediately after overtaking, it often pays to ease off a very little on the accelerator after you are well clear of the overtaken vehicle. This reduces the understeer caused by acceleration, and the car will respond to the steering wheel more quickly and more exactly.

All movements follow one another very quickly when an expert driver is overtaking in the way I have outlined and the manoeuvre is completed speedily despite the methodical planning. It is also safe because you have an opportunity to re-assess and reconsider after the car has been positioned.

Time and Distance

Overtaking must, of necessity, be achieved quickly, but it must not be rushed. There must be a smooth, cohesive plan carried through with thought and care and deliberation, albeit quickly. Remember, it takes quite a few seconds and a lot of road length to overtake some traffic which you have been following at 40 m.p.h. In an ordinary family car a driver will need 17 or 18 seconds and nearly a quarter of a mile of road to overtake three vehicles which he has been following at a steady 40 m.p.h. Faster cars with better acceleration can manage it in less time and need less road, but the driver still requires care, judgement and the right technique.

All this, of course, relates to overtaking on a two- or three-lane road, when the operation is at its most tricky. Overtaking on a dual carriageway or motorway or four-lane road is much easier, but still must be done in accordance with the system and the established rules of the road. On these roads you will need to reduce speed only if there is traffic in the offside lane or some geographical feature ahead which makes overtaking dangerous.

Geographical features include bridges over the road, especially if there is a strong wind, because there can be so much air turbulence near and under bridges that even a stable car can be shifted off course, and an overtaking driver thus affected may not have sufficient room to manoeuvre. A clump of trees close to the road, or a gap in a line of trees or buildings, can create similar problems when there is a strong cross-wind.

Dual Carriageways

Usually on wide dual roads the driver does not need to adjust speed or gear, although he must still pay careful attention to position, mirrors and signals, including horn and flasher if the vehicle being overtaken seems a little unsteady.

It is wrong and bad driving to stay permanently in the overtaking lane. On motorways with three lanes in each direction, this is the offside lane. A driver travelling fairly quickly on a motorway should occupy the middle lane normally and only move to the offside to overtake.

The middle lane is the safest lane, anyway, because you have room each side to manoeuvre if you suffer a burst tyre or if a car coming in the opposite direction crosses the middle out of control.

Trouble at Speed

Both these events are rare, so rare that many people do not consider in advance what action ought to be taken and as a result may do completely the wrong thing.

If a tyre bursts do not brake. The flat tyre will not grip and the car may slew round and be completely uncontrollable. Instead of braking, steer the car as well as you are able, lift off on the accelerator, signal that you are pulling in to the side and check your mirrors.

Do not attempt to change down or use the handbrake, because that would involve one hand off the steering wheel at a time when the biggest problem in your life will be steering the car. If it is a front tyre which has burst you may change down or use the handbrake once the car is travelling fairly slowly and in control, provided the car is rear-wheel drive. The thing is to avoid any kind of braking pressure on the wheel with the burst tyre, particularly if it is a front wheel.

The problem of a car out of control and crossing the middle of a motorway or dual carriageway is another tricky one. Imagine you are travelling along in the middle lane of a motorway with three lanes in each direction, and a car coming the other way crosses the middle. The instinctive reaction is to turn the wheel to the left, away from the other half of the road. In most cases this is the wrong thing to do. Your car and the car out of control would move along converging lines. If you turn your wheel to the right you should be able to pass on the inside and be safe.

9

Cornering

There are more wrong ideas and theories about cornering than almost anything else in driving, and unfortunately many of them are due to the way people misinterpret the sound advice in *Roadcraft*. The manual says that you should drive round a corner 'under progressive acceleration', and many people assume that this means that when you reach a corner you put your right foot hard down and turn the steering wheel. That is not what it means, and this method of cornering is wrong and dangerous.

In the chapter on balancing a car I referred to the forces which come into play once you turn the steering wheel, and I also mentioned other forces; it is now necessary to know a little more about these.

Tyre adhesion to the road surface can resist only a certain fixed amount of force. Excessive force will cause loss of adhesion, and it does not matter whether the force is from one source or a number of sources acting together. If tyre adhesion in given circumstances can withstand X amount of force, then X plus anything will cause loss of adhesion, resulting in a skid.

Dangerous Forces

There are many forces which act when a car is being driven. Acceleration and braking both bring forces into action, and most drivers must have experienced the loss of grip which can be caused by one or other of these. Wheelspin is a common example of tyres losing their grip because of excessive force applied through acceleration. In this situation so much torque is applied to the driving wheels that they are forced to turn before the car actually moves. The force pushing the wheels round is, in fact, pushing the piece of tyre in contact with the road backwards so strongly that it loses its grip and slips backwards. In mud or on a wet or slippery road it is fairly easy to reach a situation where the driving wheels just spin without the car ever moving, and the only possible way to make it move is to reduce the force being applied to the driving wheels. In very powerful cars a similar thing can happen on a dry road, resulting in clouds of smoke from burning rubber.

If you brake too hard the wheels can be locked and the car will not stop, because momentum carries it forward. The tyre in contact with the road surface again loses its grip and the car skids, usually leaving a trail of rubber on the road if dry.

These two things can happen when the car is pointing in a straight line. You can see how much easier it is to lose adhesion when there is centrifugal force pushing at the car as well.

It is obvious that going the whole way round a corner with your foot firmly down on the accelerator must reduce the ability of the driving wheels to withstand the sideways thrust of centrifugal force. Yet many people advise it and do it, very largely due to those misunderstood words 'progressive acceleration'. Racing drivers often corner in this way because they actually want to reduce rear-wheel adhesion.

I will explain why they do it, and at the same time warn you most strongly not to attempt it on any road.

On the Race-track

Most cars being driven fast under fierce acceleration will run very wide, and this is what happens in many racing cars.

So the racing driver—who nowadays is really a motoring scientist because he works within such fine limits—balances this by reducing the adhesion of the rear wheels. Once they lose their grip on the road the back end of the car starts to slide and in doing so points the nose of the car tighter into the corner. In the hands of an inexpert driver it would probably spin. In the hands of a racing or rally driver, however, the sliding at the back is so perfectly controlled that the car is moving sideways with no loss of speed whatsoever. In order to keep the front of the car on course the driver will be applying corrective steering much the same as in skid-correction. This means that he will be taking a right-hand bend steering left, which is known as 'opposite lock'. This controlled movement of the car is called a drift.

One might be excused for saying that the car is skidding. However, this is not so because, while a skid is involuntary and needs to be controlled after it has happened, a drift is created, and its limits are controlled by the driver throughout.

Not on Public Roads

There are many reasons why this must never be attempted on public roads, the most important of them being that the driver would probably lose control and kill himself or some innocent party.

Another is that it is not possible with most standard road cars. Yet another is that a drift should be regarded as a complete thing, which cannot be interrupted in the middle. Once started, it must be finished, or else you must spin or run off the road or track. A car in a drift is balanced, but it is such a delicate balance that it must not be interfered with, even by the most skilled scientist, without the risk of serious consequences. So a driver drifting a car round a corner on a public road would have absolutely no way of missing the child he did not see or the parked van that was invisible from the point where he started his cornering.

I have heard drivers boasting among themselves of practising drifting through roundabouts when the roads are empty in the early hours of the morning. This is all very well, but there is no doubt it amounts to dangerous driving, and I think it is a stupid thing to do.

But it does perhaps make a case for more areas to be made available to enthusiasts for competitive driving events, where they can improve their skill and get rid of their inhibitions.

It is certain that competitive driving tests in particular teach a great deal about car-handling generally—judgement and self discipline—the hard way.

After taking part in such a competition, even under the strictly controlled conditions imposed by the R.A.C., one always seems more content and better able to put up with the frustrations of every-day motoring.

The Vital Points

There are nine things to be borne in mind when cornering on a public road anywhere, in town or out of town. They are:

1. VISIBILITY: in cornering, as in everything in driving, you must be ruled by what you can see and must assume that there is danger lurking in any spot you cannot see.
2. ANGLE: obviously the sharper the angle the slower you must travel, as understeer (or oversteer) and centrifugal force increase as the angle sharpens.
3. SPEED: understeer (or oversteer) and centrifugal force increase with speed, as does the weight-shift towards the outside wheels. So, naturally, does stopping distance, and you must be prepared and able to stop within the distance that you can see.
4. ROAD SURFACE: a bad, slippery, gravelly, icy, wet or

pot-holed surface reduces adhesion, so the grip of the
tyres is less able to combat the forces pushing at the car.

5. UNDERSTEER (or oversteer): understeer is at its greatest
and most noticeable immediately after you turn the
steering wheel. A car travelling in a straight line wants
to go on travelling that way. No car really wants to go
round a corner, so the whole momentum and weight
keep pushing it onwards even after you turn the wheel.
The difference between the slip angles (see Chapter Four)
of front and rear wheels is greatest just after you turn
the steering wheel and before the car responds. If you
are accelerating at the same time there will be even more
force pushing the car forward, and the understeer will
be even more marked. (Oversteer also is at its greatest
just after the car responds, and for very similar reasons.)

6. WEIGHT DISTRIBUTION: braking throws weight forward to the front wheels and lightens the load over the
rear wheels so that their adhesion is reduced (see Chapter
Four). Acceleration takes weight away from the front
and throws it over the rear wheels. Centrifugal force
pushes the car outwards, shifting weight from the inside
to the outside wheels. Under braking while cornering at
speed most weight rests on the outside front wheel.
Under really fierce acceleration when cornering at speed
most weight rests on the outside rear wheel, although the
tendency is less marked than when braking. In either of
these states the car is badly unbalanced.

7. ACCELERATION FORCES: in addition to its possible
effect on understeer and oversteer and weight distribution, acceleration can reduce the adhesion of the driving
wheels, as discussed earlier in this chapter. In an understeering car with front-wheel drive harsh acceleration will
increase the understeer and reduce the adhesion at the
front, so that the car will have a marked tendency to go
straight on. In an oversteering rear-wheel-drive car the

reverse applies, and the car will tend to spin. The right amount of acceleration is good, however, and helps to stabilise the car.

8. BRAKING FORCES: apart from its deadly effect on weight distribution braking always makes some reduction in the ability of the tyres to grip. Harsh braking can lock the wheels so that all grip is lost, and if this happens while cornering all else is lost as well, including, possibly, your life.

9. CENTRIFUGAL FORCE: I have put this last because so many people put it first and give the impression that this is the only force one has to worry about. Anything moving in a circle or arc is pushed outwards by centrifugal force, which is the secret of the Wall of Death riders. Every turn can be thought of as part of the perimeter of a circle. Imagine the complete circle with a line drawn from the car to the centre. If centrifugal force took complete control, the car would shoot out of the circle at right angles to that line. This is the same direction in which understeer takes a car.

Help the Tyres

Now, I suppose it sounds impossible to make a car go round a corner safely and with any sort of speed, but it is, in fact, quite simple if you know how and do it correctly. Bear in mind that the marvellous grip of modern tyres is a great ally, so that all you have to do is to reduce or eliminate the forces which prevent the tyres doing their job.

If one is driving in town on a dry road at a legal speed many of the problems do not arise, because the speed is so low that the forces cannot become strong enough to upset the car on any ordinary corner. However, even in town the rules should be obeyed, because in that way they become second nature;

and, besides, the road may not always be dry and safe. On the open road it is imperative that all corners and bends are treated with respect and the correct procedure.

Cornering in Detail

I think the easiest way to demonstrate how to corner in a way that reduces or eliminates the dangerous forces is to describe in detail the method which I use, and taught to my police students. I will use two examples, a sharp left-hand bend on a fast open road, and a sharp right-hand bend on the same road.

The first thing to be dealt with is, as always, position. Your view round a left-hand bend is better if you keep out to the right, and this also can help to reduce the angle of the turn necessary to travel the bend. Nevertheless I do not believe in positioning the car on the crown of the road. In my opinion the great truth about that position is that you get a much clearer, much earlier and certainly much better view of the car coming the other way that is going to hit you. Personally I have no wish for that sort of view, because I have no wish to have any sort of involvement with another car.

I believe in positioning my car about three feet or so from the centre when approaching a left-hand bend because then you are fairly clear of anything coming the other way, even if the other car does cross the line. My position gives a reasonable view into the corner and also allows a good safe line round it.

Again I disagree with many people on the line that should be taken on a left-hand bend. Their teaching is that one should use a line of constant radius, in other words a perfect arc starting near the middle line, coming into the verge at the apex and finishing up almost on the middle line again. I think that is a dangerous line.

If something goes wrong it will probably happen after the car has clipped the apex and is on its way to the middle of the road. If, therefore, you have to correct a skid or deal with anything else there is only the other side of the road in which to do it. I do not need to point out the dangers of that situation.

I believe in taking a line which allows room at all times to manoeuvre in your own half of the road. The position for the bend and the approach to it are dictated by the line you intend to use, which is why I make this point now, before we have even reached the bend. If the positioning and approach are wrong the whole of your cornering will be wrong.

The line that I recommend involves braking well up to the corner while still maintaining your position not too close to the middle line. You maintain your position beyond the point where someone taking the line of constant radius would turn his steering wheel, and this means you obtain the best view ahead before you commit yourself.

The actual turn is made at a sharper angle than for a line of constant radius, and in some cases the angle of the turn may be sharper than the angle of the corner itself. So you have to make your turn at a slower speed than someone using the line of constant radius. However there are compensations, and I have never heard anyone complain that Flying Squad drivers using this line go round corners slowly.

You finish your braking well before you turn, of course, and you may have to change into a lower gear. Then you apply the drive, but just enough to maintain your speed and balance the car. This is one of the reasons why you may have changed down. If your gear is too high the engine will be straining under acceleration, and not enough power will be transmitted to balance the car. If you are in a lower gear you will be able to give exactly the amount of power you require. You remain in top gear only if your speed is sufficient for you to be able to make this power-choice in that gear.

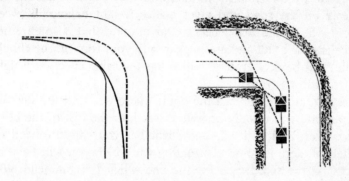

6. The diagram on the left shows the course followed on a left-hand bend by drivers using what is commonly called 'the line of constant radius'. I consider this to be a bad, unsafe and possibly slower line. The driver is committed to his angle of turn and has fixed his speed before he can see anything of what may be round the corner. He starts and finishes at the crown of the road which means that he cannot manoeuvre in his own half of the road to cope with any trouble which may be waiting just round the bend. The diagram on the right shows the line I use for a left-hand bend. Someone using the line of constant radius would have to start his turn where the first car is marked, and the broken line shows his line of vision. The later turn which I recommend allows the driver to see well into the bend before he turns the steering wheel. I like to finish the turn close to the nearside so that I have room to manoeuvre if there is a skid or obstruction. The diagram below shows the lines I use for hairpin bends, with range of vision marked.

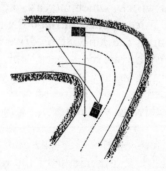

Acceleration sufficient to maintain your speed settles the car nicely on the road and gives a nice weight balance between front wheels and rear wheels. Bear in mind that if you are not accelerating at all and are in gear with your foot off the clutch, you must be decelerating, which has the same effect on weight distribution as braking.

By the time you reach the point where you turn the steering wheel you will usually be able to see into the rest of the bend or corner, and you will know whether you can go ahead or whether there is some obstruction for which you will have to stop. At the speed used for the line which I recommend, you will be able to stop within your range of vision. The speed normally used for a line of constant radius is too high for this, although in practice there is not such a vast difference. But on a line of constant radius you do not see right round the corner until a moment after your car has clipped the apex, and by then it is too late to stop.

You start to make the turn while still under moderate acceleration. If you increase your acceleration before you turn the wheel you will increase understeer (or oversteer). So you turn your wheel and then accelerate. You progress from one rate of acceleration to another, as in the misunderstood phrase 'progressive acceleration' mentioned earlier.

After you start the turn the extra drive causes more weight to shift to the rear wheels, which increases adhesion sufficiently to balance for the force applied through the accelerator.

Initially, of course, the amount of drive you apply makes very little difference to your road-speed—this shows no marked increase until you are already straightening out after the turn. The turn is sharper than for a line of constant radius and is finished more quickly, so you are able to increase your speed more quickly.

You finish the turn on the near side and you do not allow the car to move back to the middle of the road. You have all your half of the road in which to manoeuvre or correct any

This is the right distance at which to wait before overtaking. It is rather closer than the following distance, but the positioning of the car gives a good view ahead so that danger can be seen well in advance, but you are close enough to be able to take advantage of any suitable break in traffic.

Now I have moved out a little but not yet begun to close on the car ahead. This enables me to make certain that all is absolutely clear while I still have a gap to move back into if necessary. Also, one should move into position before starting to accelerate so that other drivers can see how much room is required.

I am in position and travelling in a straight line before attempting to go past.

At the moment of overtaking the cars are completely parallel and about four or five feet apart.

Drivers turning right at a crossroads should never pass in front of one another like this.

This is the effect of passing in front of one another at a crossroads or traffic lights. Each car obscures the other driver's view of oncoming traffic, and this leads to accidents. The bad habit of turning right this way is very common outside London.

This is the correct way to turn right at crossroads or traffic lights. The cars pass behind one another.

By passing behind one another each driver has a good view. Besides that, at busy traffic lights it enables more drivers to go right during a change as the leading cars begin the turn from farther across the junction.

Lanes are not marked at roundabouts, but drivers should still observe lane discipline. There are few roundabouts where cars cannot go around side by side like this.

Cars leaving roundabouts by the same exit can still do so side by side, and this is the safe and proper way.

This is an example of bad behaviour at roundabouts. The white Escort is cutting in right in front of my Rover as the driver moves needlessly and carelessly from the outside to the inside lane, in the belief that he will get round faster that way. In fact, traffic will flow faster and more smoothly if drivers observe lane discipline at roundabouts.

Here again the white Escort is cutting in right across my bonnet. There was plenty of room for him to leave in his own lane, but instead he uses two lanes in a way that could cause an accident.

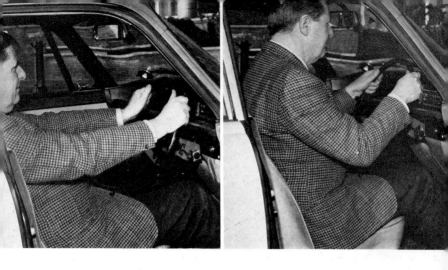

Above left. In this bad driving position the driver could only reach the top of the wheel by leaning forward, so at times he will not get full support from the seat. As a result he will have to use the steering-wheel for support, and this will mean grasping it so tightly that he will be insensitive to 'skid messages' passed through the wheel.

Above right. This second bad position is popular with learners and novices who have been taught badly. The driver gets no support from the seat, he cannot move the wheel properly and his grip will be tight and insensitive.

Below left. This shows a handy way of finding a good driving position. With your back firmly against the back of the seat you should be able to hold the top of the steering-wheel with straight arm. Once adjusted to that position drop your hands to around ten to two or a quarter to three and you should be in a comfortable, relaxed position.

Below right. This is my normal driving position, and the distance from the wheel is exactly the one using the method in the picture on the left. In my experience an improved driving position leads instantly to improved driving.

John Miles giving classroom instruction to police trainees intended for the Flying Squad and other top motoring units of the Metropolitan Police. Training was based on the police driving manual plus a series of lectures explaining and amplifying the information in the manual. In this book Mr Miles gives all the information contained both in the lectures and the manual, plus tips from his own personal experience as a driver and advanced instructor.

skid or slide which may have developed through your own carelessness. On most roads this means that the car could spin right round without crossing the centre line.

A turn executed this way has achieved every possible object. You have had good visibility before being committed to a particular course of action; you have eliminated or reduced the forces acting on the car; and you have had ample time to deal with any contingency. A turn along a line of constant radius does not fulfil these objects.

Open and Closed Bends

In many cases one finds that drivers position the car automatically for bends with little thought for what actually lies ahead. They take the attitude that since it is a left-hand bend they always must position out towards the centre line.

This is not necessarily so.

Why do you position the car? You position so that you can see more of what lies ahead, or else to maintain your speed by taking a more easy line.

Some drivers will use the same road position and speed for a bend that has a hedge close to the roadside as for a similar bend which has a fifteen-feet-wide grass verge. They are, in fact, driving with their eyes fixed on the kerbline and failing to take in the whole picture.

Others take bends well known to them with some aplomb. I have often had it said to me, 'I can take this one at 40 m.p.h.' They can, mechanically. But what would happen if the road had been dug up in their absence and, as usual, the 'Road Up' sign was propped up at the hole?

The answer to problems such as these is to drive according to certain basic flexible rules and adjust them to what you can, or cannot, see.

E.D.—4

Fast Cornering

As far as speed is concerned, I believe that the line I suggest is faster overall than the line of constant radius, although I would not argue with the fact that the line of constant radius is quicker round the actual corner.

Imagine a corner where someone using a line of constant radius can reach a speed of 40 m.p.h. without sliding or skidding or drifting. The speed for my line on that corner would be about 30–35 m.p.h. On the way into the corner my line allows later braking in complete safety, because the car remains straight for a longer period, so that a few feet would be gained. On my line the car is straight again much earlier, so that full acceleration can be used long before it would be possible with the line of constant radius, and I think this would be a telling effect overall.

Right-hand Bend

I do not believe in the line of constant radius even for a right-hand bend. Again my police line involves braking well up to the corner, changing down if necessary, applying enough drive to maintain speed, and starting the turn at a point with maximum vision round the corner. Again, of course, you progress to firmer acceleration *after* the steering-wheel has been turned.

I do not believe in going too close to the centre line in the middle of a right-hand turn, because someone coming the other way may have misjudged it and gone over the line. I prefer to go exactly as shown in the diagram.

'Progressive Acceleration'

I hope the *true* meaning of 'progressive acceleration' is clear from this. You accelerate moderately up to the moment

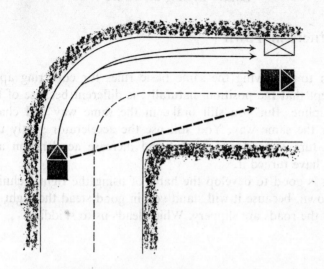

7. I do not believe in going close to the middle of the road at any time when going round a right-hand bend. The line I use is indicated here and the heavy broken line shows the field of vision before starting the turn. A driver using this line has good vision round the corner and is in a position where he can manoeuvre freely if there is any kind of obstruction.

you turn the steering-wheel and, having done so, you then progress to stronger acceleration. Speed increases after the turn. Any other kind of acceleration in road driving is nonsense.

During the approach to any corner you brake down to the speed that you decide is right for you, which is the correct and sensible thing to do. Yet some people would have us believe that you should then start accelerating quite hard again. You decide, perhaps, that the speed for the corner or bend should be 35 m.p.h. and brake down to that instinctively. So why then start accelerating so that your speed in the dangerous middle bit of the corner is 40 m.p.h.? It just does not make sense, and, in any case, why argue with your own judgement?

Corners in Town

In town driving the same basic rules for cornering apply, except that the position, naturally, is different because of lane discipline. But you still brake in the same way and change gear the same way. You still use the accelerator gently until you turn your steering-wheel and increase acceleration after you have turned it.

It is good to develop the habit of using the right technique in town, because it will stand you in good stead the night you find the roads are slippery. Which leads us to skidding.

10

❖❖❖

Skidding

Cars do not skid by themselves. The driver makes them skid. Nobody gets much sympathy from me if he tries to explain an accident by saying: 'It wasn't my fault. The car skidded.'

The car would not have skidded if the driver had been doing the right thing, and besides this, if he knew his driving techniques properly he would be able to correct the skid. It is possible to drive a car safely, albeit slowly, along a road so icy that people find it difficult to stand. Yet bad drivers sometimes lose control and skid on ordinary dry roads, and drivers who are not quite so bad quite frequently lose control and skid on wet roads that should be perfectly safe.

Skid Conditions

There are certain conditions and situations which make skids more likely to occur if the driver is unwary, and it can be taken as a basic rule that such things as water, snow, ice, leaves, gravel, mud, vegetables (especially sugar beet) fallen from lorries will increase the risk.

Even something like a wet newspaper could present a risk. Skidding situations occur particularly when any of the forces dealt with in Chapters Four and Nine are brought into play, usually during cornering, braking and accelerating.

In Britain the most common element to create skid conditions is rain, and a few facts and figures may show why.

Tyres on Wet Roads

A new tyre of modern tread and design has only half its normal grip on the road at 60 m.p.h. in rain. A half-worn tyre or a tyre of outdated design has only a quarter of its normal grip in the same conditions.

The tyre can only grip to the road, not to the rain lying on the surface, so the tread pattern must disperse the water from the road before it can grip, and the water is shifted through the grooves in the tread. At 60 m.p.h. in moderate rain the tyre has to disperse eight pints of water per second before it can grip to the road. Each element of the tread pattern is in contact with the road for just one-hundredth-and-fiftieth of a second at that speed, which is not very long in which to disperse its share of water and grip to the road. It is, in fact, about half as long as it takes to blink your eye.

If the tyre cannot shift the water it can only ride on top of it, and that is when the car starts aquaplaning. This is likely to happen at high speed in heavy rain on worn tyres, but on good tyres even very fast cars will not reach aquaplaning speed in anything but freak storm conditions. If tyres are bald, however, a car can aquaplane on a wet road at about 50 m.p.h. Once aquaplaning starts the driver cannot steer or brake or accelerate, and there will be almost nothing but wind resistance to reduce his speed.

Skids from Braking

Apart from aquaplaning, which is rare, cars seldom skid when travelling in a straight line, and when it does happen the main cause is braking. This sort of skid is caused by travelling at an excessive speed for where you are, forcing you to brake too harshly for the road conditions.

If you brake too hard the wheels will lock and the car will slide forward. If the road is slippery for any reason then this is much more likely to happen, but there will be no skid as long as the wheels keep turning. The grip of the tyres to the road must always be stronger than the grip of the brake pads to the discs, or the linings to the drums. As soon as the brake-grip becomes stronger than the tyre-grip the wheels will lock and there will be a skid during which the car will be uncontrollable.

There is a demonstration of this which I am fond of, but it needs either a skid-road or skid-pan, which has an extremely slippery surface. In this demonstration I ask the student to brake as hard as he can and then turn the steering-wheel. The braking locks the wheels, and turning the steering-wheel has no effect at all on the direction in which the car is travelling. It keeps going in a straight line.

But once the brake pedal is released the wheels start turning again and the car responds to the steering and starts to change direction.

In fact, the change of direction can be so sudden that the back of the car will skid as the car turns into the corner.

This demonstrates two things. The first is that a car is absolutely out of control when the wheels are locked. The second is that, when a skid is caused by harsh braking, correction can only begin by releasing the brake pedal.

This sort of skid can occur during an emergency on a dry road when the driver brakes too hard, but whether the road is wet or dry the only way to deal with it is to lift off the brake. A skidding car is not slowing down efficiently, and even during an emergency stop, if you begin to skid you must lift off briefly and then brake again more gently.

The other normal types of skid occur when cornering, and these come in two kinds, front wheel and rear wheel. The rare wheel skid is the more common and, fortunately, the easier to deal with.

Rear Wheel Skids

In a rear wheel skid the back end of the car breaks away and slides outwards. It is as if the back were trying to overtake the front, and that is exactly what will happen if you do nothing about it, and you will finish up looking at the place you have just left, unless you hit something first. This sort of skid is caused by excessive speed, by coarse steering or by harsh acceleration. It may also be caused by sharp deceleration or braking which throws weight forward, reducing adhesion at the back.

If it happens while rounding a left-hand bend or corner the back moves out to the right, and the normal method of correction is to lift off the accelerator and turn the steering-wheel to the right. Do not touch the brake or clutch. This, if done promptly enough, will correct the skid, and when all four wheels are pointing in the same direction you may start accelerating again. On a right-hand bend you turn the steering wheel to the left.

This basic method of correction is effective for all rear wheel skids however caused, and the only problems are that you might act too late or you might over-correct the steering, which can cause a skid in the other direction if the road is really slippery. Only experience in skid-control will help you overcome these problems, and until you have acquired experience either on a skid-pan or skid-road or a piece of slippery private road you should treat all skid conditions with caution.

Someone who is expert and sensitive can use other methods of correcting a rear wheel skid. Such a driver may feel the skid almost before it starts, and his experience and sensitivity will tell him what to do. If, say, it was caused by excessive accelera-

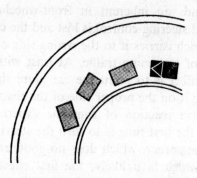

8. In a rear-wheel skid the back end of the car breaks away with the effect that the car points more sharply into the corner. The cure is to turn the steering wheel to opposite lock—in other words, if the skid occurs on a left-hand bend the wheel should be turned to the right. If it occurs on a right-hand bend it should be turned to the left.

tion he could gain control by easing off the accelerator pedal. If caused by weight distribution, he might deal with it by greater pressure on the accelerator, but there are few other than professional drivers who have the experience, skill, speed and sensitivity to do this properly.

The normal rules for correcting a rear wheel skid, therefore, are:

1. Remove foot from accelerator pedal. Do not touch brake or clutch.
2. On a left-hand corner turn the steering to the right. On a right-hand corner turn the steering-wheel to the left.
3. Once the skid is under control straighten the steering and accelerate gently when all four wheels are in line.

Front Wheel Skids

Front wheel skids are more dangerous and more difficult to control. They are caused by excessive speed or by excessive acceleration and are inherent in front-wheel-drive cars. In this sort of skid steering-control is lost and the car goes almost straight on, which carries it to the wrong side of the road and into the path of oncoming traffic. At least with a rear wheel skid the first effect is to point the car more sharply into the corner, keeping it on the proper side of the road.

The instinctive reaction of someone experiencing a front wheel skid for the first time is to turn the steering-wheel more sharply into the corner, which does no good at all. If the car did respond, which is unlikely, the first effect would be to increase centrifugal force, and the back of the car would break away, making things worse.

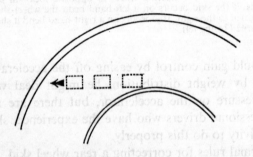

9. In a front-wheel skid the car tends to go straight on, as indicated in this diagram. This type of skid is most common in a front-wheel drive car and is extremely dangerous and difficult to correct. The methods which may be used are explained in this chapter.

Only by eliminating or nullifying the effect of centrifugal force by loss of speed can the everyday driver control a front wheel skid; therefore it is dealt with in the following way:

1. Remove foot from accelerator pedal.
2. Straighten the steering, even for a moment.
3. Turn the steering-wheel smoothly again in the direction in which you hope to travel.

In my opinion this is not a very satisfactory way in which

to deal with this type of skid, because it does not always work, and even when it does work you may have to use both sides of the road.

Skid Training

I am a great believer in teaching people about skids on skid-roads or skid-pans, because skids are a major cause of accidents. Not only does instruction help a driver cope with future skids, but it also teaches him so much about the causes of skidding that he is less likely to have a skid thereafter. He can feel one a long way off and do something about it before it happens.

I wish every local authority in Britain shared my views on skid training, because then they might consider skid-control instruction centres just as important to road safety as zebra crossings. Every driver should have an opportunity to receive instruction and practice in skid-control.

The more serious and sensitive students would learn to create their own skids and to control them. Learning to create a skid to within precise limits will give confidence and teach more quickly than any other method the causes of skidding and the ways to keep the car where it should be.

You do find that rally and competition drivers will often deliberately put a car sideways to slow it down, and at the same time point it into a corner. This must not be done on a road, of course, but it serves to show that because the car is not straight there is no need to give up.

Just remember that, generally speaking, you will not skid until you find yourself going too fast with too little space and too little time to do what has to be done. Then your use of the steering, brakes and accelerator will become harsh and a skid is almost inevitable.

When you are 'keeping up with the Joneses' just have a look at their dents and bumps, and pause to consider whether the next bump he gets will be when he hits you, and whether it might be a good idea to keep clear and drive at your own pace.

Other Techniques

A valuable skid technique which can be learned fairly quickly is what competition drivers call the 'hand-brake turn'. This is a method of making a car spin round, and someone who is expert can control the amount of spin. The driver simply turns his steering-wheel sharply to transfer weight and pulls hard on the hand-brake to lock the rear wheels. In a rear-wheel-drive car he should also put his foot on the clutch.

A car can be made to spin right round to point in the opposite direction in not much more than its own length and in less than half the width of a normal road by this method. A car spun in this way comes to a complete halt. It is probably the quickest way of stopping a car other than by hitting something solid.

I think a driver should try to acquire every possible skill which will make him better, more confident and safer. Advanced skid techniques can do this, and some can be learned remarkably quickly by a driver with aptitude.

It is quite common to start someone off on skid instruction by taking him round a skid-pan or skid-road corner at 10 miles an hour, and find he loses control. An hour later he can go round the same corner with good control at 20 or 25 m.p.h. And after another hour he can be using hand-brake turns as a method of stopping which might be handy when confronted by trouble on an icy road.

Every driver should have the opportunity to acquire such skills; *whether he ever has to use them has nothing to do with it;* these skills lie in reserve against the time he needs them.

11

Braking

Stopping a car is perhaps even more important than making it go. If you cannot stop you have no right to go, and I am sure everyone would agree with that. Yet many people do not know how to stop or slow down correctly. They endeavour to do it by using the gears instead of the brakes, under the false idea that this is good driving.

The brakes are designed to make a car slow down and stop, and the gears are designed to help it speed up and go. Each should be used always for the designed purpose.

Not on the Gears

The fallacy that it is right and good and clever and safe driving to slow on the gears dates back to the days of cable brakes, which frequently did not give even braking on both sides of the car. Because of this drivers developed the technique of changing down to slow down, especially on slippery roads. This gave less effective but even braking on the rear wheels. Nowadays brakes are perfectly balanced so that the problem does not arise, which makes the old solution unnecessary.

The brakes operate on all four wheels, and if you are to have full braking you need all four tyres working for you. In most cars 60 per cent of the total braking is done by the front wheels, which means that the maximum possible braking effect through

109

the rear wheels is about 40 per cent. So, whatever the conditions, you cannot get even half the possible braking effect with rear wheels only, and using the gears you are not likely to get more than about a quarter of the full braking potential of the car. On a really slippery road it is easier to lock the rear wheels by changing down than by gentle braking, and it is more difficult to unlock them.

Apart from all this, you can judge your braking distance if you use the brakes. You cannot do it correctly if you use the gears. The Highway Code tells you that at 50 m.p.h. you need 125 feet to bring the car to a standstill from the moment you touch the brake, and that most people need another 50 feet to realise that braking is necessary and transfer a foot from the accelerator to the brake. If you use the gears, how far will the car travel before you have changed down? And how far will it travel before you have stopped? I do not know the answer, and I am sure you do not know it either.

Many people reduce speed for corners and roundabouts by using the gears and apply last-minute braking with the brakes. This is bad driving and is a complete reversal of the rules in the carefully planned and well-tried system for car-control. I have found that people who use this method have very little or no forward planning. They perhaps see a roundabout, but that is all they see. They change down and come into the hazard—often too fast—under braking and find that they cannot go because of traffic. Then they realise that the gear they chose some way back is anything but the correct one and have to put that right at the last moment. The methodical process may be slower on the way in; it's faster on the way out. Brake first; change gear later.

If Brakes Fail

Some who argue that you should change gear first claim that you are safer if your brakes fail, because you are already in gear with braking effect, but this is not a valid argument. If your brakes do fail then the earlier you know the better for you, because you can take emergency action sooner.

Complete brake failure is quite rare and is becoming more rare as dual braking systems become standard on more and more cars. The usual cause when it does happen is loss of hydraulic fluid, and there is not much one can do to prevent this, apart from routine servicing. It is possible, however, to buy quite cheaply a device which turns on a warning light when the fluid in the reservoir disappears, which is an effective warning of loss of fluid generally and enables you to take emergency action at once.

If you do lose your brakes you will have to slow on the hand-brake and the gears. It is best to use the hand-brake first and then change down quickly into as low a gear as possible.

Braking Distance Formula

Every good driver should know his braking distances, and those given in the Highway Code are useful, although a well-braked car will stop in shorter distances on good, dry roads. There is a simple formula for working out the Highway Code braking distances for speeds in round figures. You just multiply the total speed by the first figure and divide by two. Thus, the braking distance for 30 m.p.h. is 30 times three, making 90, divided by two, giving 45 feet. The distance for 60 m.p.h. is 60 multiplied by six, making 360, divided by two, giving 180 feet. This does not include the thinking distance, which is the time it takes to react to trouble and place your foot on the brake pedal, but for the average person this is one foot for every mile per hour.

Stopping

It is quite a simple matter to bring a car to a halt smoothly without jerking the passengers forward.

When you brake firmly weight is moved forward, and so are the passengers. If you hold the brake on hard until the car completely stops the car levels out again quite sharply, and so do the passengers.

By braking in good time initially it should be possible to ease off for the last yard or two before stopping, thus allowing the front of the car to rise and level off. A gentle application of the brake is then enough to bring the car to a halt.

12

Bad Weather Driving

The weather is never so bad that a car cannot be driven safely, as long as you exercise caution, skill and good sense. I can say this with some authority, because before I became a police driving instructor I spent quite a few years driving wireless cars in London; and wireless cars have to carry on duty in all weathers, as at such times crime tends to increase rather than diminish.

I think that the worst sort of driving weather is fog, especially freezing fog, but even then the driver can do a lot to make things easier for himself.

Bad Visibility

In any conditions that reduce visibility, and that includes heavy snow, rain and darkness as well as fog, the first thing the driver must ascertain is that nothing besides the weather is hampering his vision. So he should see that the windows, particularly the windscreen, are completely clean inside and out. Drivers who wear spectacles should make sure that they also are clean. I am always amazed at the number of bespectacled drivers who forget this.

In fog many drivers are afraid to allow air to enter the car through the heater/de-mister system because they are worried about fog going into the car. This worry is unnecessary, and as much air as possible should be pulled in through the de-mister system to keep the inside of the windscreen free from steam. The heater/de-mister has a filter built into it, and this removes most fog particles on the way through the system so that practically none reaches the interior of the car. (This filter should be cleaned periodically, by the way; otherwise the heater will grow steadily less effective.)

Windscreen wipers are required in heavy fog and the washer should be used liberally as well, because the outside of the screen can become dirty at a slow rate which may pass un-noticed. The driver may think the fog is thickening while in fact it may be thinning, if only he could see through the glass. I always put a small amount of additive in my washer bottle to keep the 'traffic film' of grease off the outside of the screen, and I clean the inside of all my windows regularly with one of the commercial cleaners to remove nicotine, which clings like tar.

Fog Lights

The next problem in fog and thickly falling snow is the use of lights. Headlights on full beam do nothing, except reflect back and dazzle the driver. Dipped headlights are better, and modern fog lights are best of all, but they must be placed correctly.

In daylight fog or heavy snow dipped headlights should be used, not sidelights. The main aim in daylight is to be seen by other traffic and pedestrians, and if the fog is thick enough to merit lights they must be headlights. In that sort of fog the outline of the car is visible long before sidelights.

Planning

In fog I believe it is always best to keep to main roads if possible, and preferably to roads that you know. Right turns should be avoided where this can be done, even if it means going a mile further and round a roundabout. If in a convoy of traffic do not be tempted to overtake and go into the lead. Drivers behind the leader can always see better because the movement of the leader's car clears away some of the fog. So visibility is never as good for the leader as for the followers.

The most important rule in fog, however, is: Drive slowly. You must always drive within your range of visibility, and that applies in fog as much as it applies on a bright sunny day.

One of the difficulties when there is no traffic ahead is in having no focal point. One's eyes are constantly searching and one cannot determine just how far he can see ahead. At times like this try not to lean forward in the seat and strain. Relax if you can and blink occasionally, and you will see a lot better. By straining the tendency is to stare fixedly ahead, and gradually your eyes will fix themselves on to the one thing you can see clearly, the bonnet of the car.

Ice and snow are not such great hazards as many people imagine, especially if you have had some skid-control training. Planning and care reduce the hazards for everyone, and both are essential. You should plan your equipment and you should plan your route, taking every kind of risk into account.

Prepare for Winter

Winter preparations should include selecting some extra equipment to carry in the car, and every motorist should carry such equipment even if he has no intention of attempting to drive in really bad weather. The weather may arrive unexpectedly.

Some sort of digging tool, like a spade, or even a trowel, should be carried in case the car gets stuck in snow. A small bag of sand or grit or sawdust is very handy to put under driving wheels which will not grip enough to make the car move away. But do not forget to roll the car on to it before attempting to move off. A plastic windscreen cleaner is a definite 'must', and this is the cheapest and probably the most efficient way of removing ice and snow from windows and lights. Chains are much ignored nowadays, but they are still as effective as ever and should be carried if you plan a lot of winter motoring. Make sure, however, that you know how to fit them and practise during the summer.

Before winter starts—about the time when anti-freeze is added—you should have the thermostat in the cooling system checked and, if necessary, changed to a winter one. Also, make sure your tyres are in good condition.

If there is any likelihood of ice or snow any journey should be planned carefully. A few minutes with the map, and your memory should help to avoid difficult hills. Usually main roads are best in these conditions because they are the first to receive grit or sand treatment. Little-used country lanes are good too. The surfaces are usually rough enough to allow a reasonable grip on ice. They are usually very negotiable after snow, because snow that has not been disturbed much causes little difficulty. Minor roads should be avoided, as they have enough traffic to pack the snow and make it slippery, but not enough to merit early sanding.

Starting on Ice and Snow

Moving away is often the most difficult part of driving on slippery roads, and there is absolutely no point in sitting in a car with the driving wheels spinning and the car remaining stationary. This simply results in some of the ice or snow under the driving wheels being melted, which makes that part even more slippery.

You should let in the clutch very gently and smoothly and use little acceleration when attempting to move off. If the car will not move forward in first gear, try it in second. If that does not work try reversing, because you may be able to move to a part with more grip to help you forwards. In a rear-wheel-drive car the front wheels should be kept straight, but in a front-wheel-drive car you can try turning them a little, as the change of angle may result in improved grip.

If you still cannot move away, throw some of your grit or sand or sawdust around and under the driving wheels. If you have none, try scraping some of the grit from under the wings. If that fails, take out the mats and tuck them under and in front of the driving wheels. You may be able to drive out on top of them and then you can stop and pick them up. But if you apply a violent drive to the wheels the mats may just shoot backwards.

Frozen door locks can be a nuisance. You can deal with this either by holding a match or cigarette lighter under the lock until it de-freezes or by warming the key in the same way so that it melts its own way into the lock.

Driving on Slippery Roads

Driving on slippery roads requires caution and gentleness. Any harsh movements of steering, brake or accelerator may cause a skid, so use all controls smoothly. Stay in as high a gear as possible, particularly going uphill, because the reduced torque in high gears makes you less likely to cause wheelspin by rough acceleration. Leave as much room as possible between your car and the one in front, especially going up or down hills, and ignore drivers who overtake and slip in ahead of you. Do not be tempted to drive faster than you consider safe.

In the chapter on Braking I have stressed that in all conditions the brakes are the best, surest and safest method of slowing down, but I repeat it here because of that old claim that on slippery roads one should slow on the gears. This is just not true, and you are much more likely to lock your driving wheels and skid by slowing on the gears than by using the brakes.

If you find it difficult to brake on a slippery road without locking wheels, try pumping the foot-brake up and down. This gives quite effective stopping power. Maximum braking comes just before the wheels lock, and the pumping technique may produce lots of moments when the wheels are locked, but it also gives lots of moments of maximum braking for the conditions.

On sunny days after frost, watch out for patches of ice in the shadow of trees or houses or even hedges, because these can be dangerous.

There is a theory that on slippery roads or when you are stuck in the snow or mud you should reduce tyre pressures. I tried this years ago when I was badly stuck during a rally and I did not manage to get unstuck this way, so I decided that there was something wrong with the theory. Recent research has proved that I was right, because it has been established that normal tyre pressures are best, even when stuck. The reason is that, when the tyres are hard, the air inside forces the tread pattern down into the mud or snow so that you get maximum possible grip for the conditions.

13

Traffic Driving

Most British motorists do 90 per cent of their driving in towns. They learned to drive in towns, they passed their tests in towns, they work and shop in towns, so they should all be expert at driving in town traffic. Alas and unfortunately this just is not so. I have no idea how some of them manage to keep their licences.

Some women drivers appear to be more interested in shop windows than in the traffic situations ahead of them, and some men may pay more attention to the girls on the pavements than to the cars on the road. People who cannot control their eyes cannot control their cars.

Discipline

Both your mind and your movements must be disciplined for town driving, otherwise you will cause and be involved in a lot of trouble. If you cannot drive in a disciplined way, go to the dodgems at a fairground and enjoy yourself, but leave motor-cars alone, please.

Discipline is one of those unfortunate words tainted with suggestions of interminable Army drill and with undertones of Fascism and Communism, but as far as driving is concerned it simply means the method of driving which is legal, safe and

119

sensible and causes minimum inconvenience to all road users, including yourself. That way the traffic keeps flowing.

Many undisciplined drivers who rush about in towns simply hurry from traffic jam to traffic jam because they are constantly being caught in the wrong lane. They do not take care to plan their moves ahead and note the signs which indicate what other drivers may do.

Following-distance

One of the secrets of good planning in towns is to follow at the right distance. Most cars in traffic are too close together, with the result that only the car at the front of the line has a good view ahead. I often see cars close behind lorries and vans, and the car drivers cannot possibly see anything of the traffic situations towards which they are heading. This not only prevents correct planning; it is positively dangerous because of the braking problem created.

Many drivers do not seem to realise the braking danger of following too close to the car in front in traffic. It arises mainly because emergency stops are rare on crowded roads, which means that gentle braking is all that is needed for most situations. Drivers develop the habit of braking gently.

So what happens if the vehicle ahead does have to make an emergency stop? Unless the driver behind is far enough back to see the true situation he will probably not brake hard enough. He will see the brake lights on the vehicle ahead and assume subconsciously that the traffic is going to slow down. He will use the normal gentle braking and then realise too late that he should have been braking hard for an emergency.

Signals

The importance of signalling cannot be overstated, and each

signal must be early, it must be clear, it must be accurate and it must be cancelled as soon as the advertised manoeuvre is completed.

Other motorists will plan their driving by your signals. If you are giving a left-turn signal as you approach a junction a driver waiting to emerge from the left may assume that it is safe to come out—which it probably will be if you really intend turning left. But it will be decidedly unsafe if you intend going straight on.

Bad signalling, especially at busy times, upsets people, and a driver who is upset may lose his temper and become dangerous. This sort of thing can be caused by a common signalling fault at traffic lights. Many drivers waiting to turn right at red lights give no signal until after the lights have changed, by which time motorists behind may have assumed that the car will be going straight on. So the motorists behind are irritated. The irritation would have been avoided if the driver waiting to turn right had given his signal before he even stopped at the lights, and allowed following drivers to choose another lane.

Another common fault is that some people think a signal gives them the right to do whatever they want to do, and to hell with everybody else. A signal gives you no rights whatsoever. Suppose you have to move from the nearside to the offside lane and give a signal. If you assume that you may change lane instantly you are guilty of bad and dangerous driving. You must wait until there is a break in the traffic or until another driver signifies that you may slip in ahead of him.

Roundabouts

Roundabouts provide some of the worst examples of bad signalling. Lots of drivers signal a right turn, then a left turn and go straight on. They have so many winking lights that their cars look like commercial Christmas trees.

The procedure for signalling at roundabouts is as follows:

1. Turning left. Give a left-turn signal while approaching the roundabout and maintain the signal until you have exited.
2. Turning right. To regularise the system the Highway Code now suggests that one approaches in the right-hand lane using the right-hand indicator until one is in the roundabout still keeping to the right-hand lane. Give a left-turn signal when opposite to the exit before the one you require.

The only signal absolutely necessary at a roundabout is the one indicating when and where you intend to exit. After all, if there is a roundabout in the road there is nothing you can do but go round it. By laying down a precise procedure in the Highway Code the Ministry of Transport hope there will be one rule for everyone.

Lane discipline is another vexing question at roundabouts. Many drivers seem to think that roundabouts are a free-for-all where lanes do not exist.

If engineers have planned a nice, wide road with two lanes in each direction it is reasonable to suppose that they planned the roundabouts so that cars could go round two abreast. This is, in fact, the case with nearly every roundabout. The lanes are not marked with white lines, but they exist all the same. A driver who approaches a roundabout in the nearside lane and straightens his line round the island so that he almost touches it and then exits in the nearside lane again has, in fact, changed lanes twice, which is dangerous if the man on his offside expects him to keep in lane.

If you are turning left you should approach in the nearside lane and keep to that lane throughout. If you are going straight on you can approach in either nearside or offside lane and you should keep to your chosen lane throughout. If you are going right you should approach in the offside lane, keep in

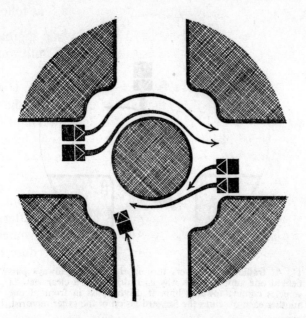

10. Lane drill is important at roundabouts, although many British motorists ignore it completely. The two cars on the left are able to enter the roundabout side by side and exit together quite comfortably and correctly. On the right one vehicle enters the roundabout in one lane, then cuts across in front of another to change lane. Then the vehicle entering from the extreme right also cuts across to the inside. This kind of behaviour is common at roundabouts, but it is incorrect and dangerous.

that lane (the one nearest to the island) round the roundabout and exit in the offside lane.

If more people followed these simple rules there would be less trouble at roundabouts and traffic would flow more smoothly.

Turning Right at Crossroads

The majority of drivers in London use the correct technique for turning right at crossroads and traffic lights, but drivers outside London seem to do it wrongly. I cannot imagine why.

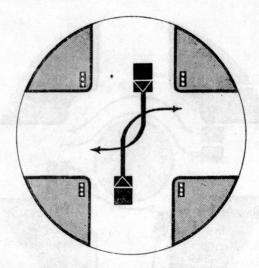

11. At traffic lights drivers turning right should always pass behind one another. This way each driver has a clear view of vehicles coming towards him. If drivers pass in front of one another each obscures the forward vision of the other motorist.

If you are turning right at this sort of junction you should go straight ahead to the farthest point from which it is possible to make the turn. At traffic lights this allows at least a couple more cars to get through the lights and wait behind you. If drivers coming the other way intend to turn right—and take up the corresponding positions—you pass behind their vehicles and they pass behind yours. This allows full vision of cars coming the other way.

If vehicles turning right pass in front of one another each obscures the vision of the other. At traffic lights it also limits the number of vehicles which can get through when the lights change.

Parking

Many drivers find it difficult or impossible to reverse into a parking space, and this is usually because they start off wrongly.

You should begin with your vehicle alongside but two or three feet clear of the vehicle at the front of the gap. You should be able to reverse straight into any space which is four feet longer than your car. If the space is smaller than that you may need two movements, one in reverse, and then one forward.

By taking the rear of your car just past the rear of the vehicle at the front of the gap you will be able to turn in at the earliest possible moment, and no space will be wasted.

If you have to reverse into a garage or opening regularly, choose permanent things to position on. You may find it difficult once the dahlias have died off if you used them.

I remember once moving the marker-posts used for a police reversing test, leaving the same distance between them. The students had great difficulty and in fact made quite a mess of things. I discovered they had been using some goal-posts on the sports-field to position on. It was then only one week away from the cricket season!

14

Motorway Driving

Motorways are fast and safe, but many of the drivers on them are fast and unsafe; or slow and unsafe; or just plain unsafe. The thing that makes them so, whether fast or slow, is that they do not obey the essential rules of law and good sense for motorway driving.

Motorways are safe because they are wide, they do not have two-way traffic, and there are no traffic lights or roundabouts or crossroads. They are fast for the same reasons. The very absence of these hazards creates new dangers, the most important of which are boredom and drowsiness, although there are many others.

Most drivers reach higher speeds on motorways than at any other time in their motoring lives, and this may strain their judgement, their thought processes and their cars. It is usual to advise people that they should not venture on motorways unless they and their cars are in good, serviceable condition, which is rather poor advice as it suggests they may travel on other roads when they and their cars are not in good condition.

Check First

I prefer to think and advise that nobody should drive on any road if any half of the car/driver partnership is not fit for use, but I also think that before going on a motorway a driver should confirm that all is well by stopping at a garage. It is advisable to have plenty of petrol because fast driving eats it up at an unpopular rate, so every driver should top up his tank before embarking on a motorway journey.

At the garage he should also check his oil, washer bottle, radiator water level, lights, windscreen wipers and tyre pressures. Ideally tyre pressures should be checked when the tyres are cold, as heat makes the air inside expand, increasing pressures. Tyre manufacturers obviously allow for this when selecting the pressures they recommend, so it is in order for tyres to seem hard when hot, as long as the car is balanced evenly over the wheels. Quite apart from this, tyre pressures should be increased for prolonged hard driving, and I would suggest an increase of about four pounds all round before commencing the journey.

At the garage the driver should get out and have a walk around in the fresh air, as this will freshen him and may also reveal touches of cramp or stiffness that could interfere with his control of the car.

If the driver is a good motorist nothing need be done as a result of most of the checks. A good motorist always ensures that the water and oil levels are correct and that his lights, etc., work, and he will use a driving position that reduces the risk of stiffness to the minimum.

The Route

Another important preparation for motorway driving is a study of your route. Although all motorways are well sign-posted it is not uncommon for a careless driver to join one by the wrong entrance and find himself going the wrong way. Similarly drivers often leave at the wrong point, or overshoot the exit they require.

You should know in advance the names of the major towns or cities near the motorway in the direction in which you wish to travel, and you should know the number of the exit you require. You can miss signposts on a motorway because of a pack of heavy lorries, but if you know the exit number you will be unlikely to make a mistake of any sort.

Joining the Motorway

The slip roads giving access to motorways have two lanes leading to a single acceleration lane on the same level as the motorway, and part of it. It is important to be in the left-hand lane of the slip road just before you reach the acceleration lane.

The acceleration lane, although geographically part of the motorway, must not be considered a motorway lane carrying certain rights of way. The right of way belongs entirely to traffic in the other lanes, and the acceleration lane is there so that you may adjust your speed to that of traffic in the nearside lane, which will enable you to move into any suitable gap without inconvenience to anyone. If there is no such gap, or if you fail to adjust your speed correctly, you must give way and stop if necessary.

On the Motorway

Motorway driving can produce boredom and drowsiness, and motorists may become unaware of the speeds at which they are travelling. All these can combine to make drivers do or attempt things they would not consider on normal roads. During a long drive on any motorway—or autobahn or auto-route or autostrada or whatever you like to call it—a motorist has nothing to relieve the monotony. There is nothing but good road with gentle curves and other vehicles travelling fairly quickly. There are no houses or pedestrians or cyclists to help show the speed at which he is travelling. There are none of the normal hazards to make him think and act, so the driver may be lulled into a lethargic state and cease to be aware. This is dangerous.

The two most common faults in motorway driving are bunching and travelling too close to the car ahead. The bunching danger, alas, has been aggravated by the 70 m.p.h. limit on motorways, but even so it would not be quite such a danger if drivers remembered the correct following distance for their speed. The correct distance, as I have mentioned in the chapter on overtaking, is 30 feet for 30 m.p.h. and one extra yard for every extra mile per hour. The distance for 70 m.p.h., therefore, is 30 feet plus forty yards, making 150 feet.

Many drivers who would allow the right distance on ordinary roads forget about it on motorways, mainly because they lose the sensation of speed. Seventy miles an hour does not feel fast on a motorway—and in my opinion it is not fast on a motorway—so some drivers do not realise they are travelling at that speed.

Another cause of cars driving too close to one another is that some drivers just do not think about the distance they should allow. A man may drive normally at 40 or 50 m.p.h. on a trunk road and never go any faster unless he is on a motorway. Then he may increase his speed by 15 or 20 m.p.h. but allow no more than his customary distance between his car and the one in front; and that distance may be too short even for his usual speed.

One often sees vehicles on motorways with only one car's length between them—and that means about 15 feet or so. That is suicidal and almost homicidal. The lack of thought which causes such things is part of the motorway madness that arises from the monotony of driving on good roads.

E.D.—5

Drowsiness

Drowsiness on motorways arises from similar things, and definite steps must be taken to fight against it. It is best to have windows closed on motorways because of the tiring effect of wind noise and the dangers of dust coming through the window, but the car must have fresh air nevertheless. Naturally that comes in through the heater system, possibly helped by the blower, but you must be careful not to make the car interior too warm.

Before you join the motorway you may be driving along with a window open and the heater warming the inside of the car. Once that window is closed the car interior will become too hot unless you alter the heater setting to reduce the temperature of air coming into the car. Remember also the dangers of pressurisation, mentioned earlier in the book. So, if your car does not have air escape vents you must leave one window open a millimetre or so, or else you must slow down periodically and open a window fully for a few seconds. If you decide on the latter course, you should slow down before you take a hand off the wheel to open a window.

It is not good to drive for long periods at a fixed speed, because the unchanging note of the engine can have a hypnotic effect which will make you drowsy. Vary your motorway speed to combat this.

I think a car radio is a good safety device for motorway-type driving, provided it is used only for music programmes and that the right kind of music is being played. In some countries there are programmes designed with the motorist in mind, and they never play consecutive records with the same rhythm. Nowadays BBC programmes often have whole batches of pop records with almost identical beats, and this may produce the same sort of dangerous hypnosis as a fixed engine sound. It is time they reserved one channel for sweet music less likely to batter one's senses. The motorist needs relaxing, not in-furiating.

Lane discipline is as important as ever on motorways, and if you wish to change lanes you must use mirrors and signals correctly, and that means early signalling. The offside lane must be regarded purely as an overtaking lane, and you should not be in it unless you are in an overtaking situation.

Overtaking

If you are overtaking properly and in the offside lane, do not allow yourself to be flustered or your plans altered by a driver who comes rushing up behind flashing his lights and sounding his horn and trying to tell you to get off the face of the earth. Complete your manoeuvre and then move over so that he may pass.

If in the process of overtaking you come up to someone who is also in the overtaking lane in preparation for passing a vehicle, be patient. You may flash your headlights to make sure he knows you are there, and he may possibly decide that he can move over to the left and let you pass before he over-takes, but do not try to blow him off the road with your horn. An irritable driver with a bad attitude may be so annoyed tha he will be made ten times worse.

It is stupid to expect him to move over behind a slower-moving vehicle to let you pass. This is the beginning of con-fusion.

Wet Road Hazards

Headlights can become so dirt-spattered on wet motorways that they lose power, and tail lights can become almost invisible, so on a wet night you should stop sometimes in a service area and see if they need cleaning. It may be unpleasant in heavy rain, but an accident as a result of poor headlights or invisible rear lights would be even more unpleasant.

Most motorways are built on a higher level than the surrounding countryside to keep them free from the typical British undulations which would stop you having a good long view ahead. This is a good thing, but it does create a wind problem, because it leaves the road more exposed. Motorways rarely if ever have hedges to give any shelter, which leaves the solution of the problem entirely in the hands of drivers.

Strong Winds

I have mentioned before that during windy weather bridges, clumps of trees, buildings and heavy lorries may all have unpleasant turbulence near to them so that care is needed. I dealt with this in the chapter on overtaking, because it was appropriate there, but there is another wind problem which drivers must consider.

If there is a strong cross-wind you may have to use the steering-wheel to lean the car into it, especially in vehicles that are easily affected by winds. If the wind is blowing from the left you may be steering slightly to the left, in fact, to counteract the wind force. Remove the wind, and the car will go off course. Bridges and other windbreakers can do just that, so you must be prepared for a steering adjustment at such times, and you should note possible windbreakers by the roadside as well as on or over the road.

Motorways carry more heavy goods vehicles than any other roads, because lorry drivers often find it quicker to take the long way round by motorway than to go direct on A and B class roads. And where there are lorries carrying goods there is the danger that a piece of the load may fall off. The greater the number of lorries the greater the risk, so watch out for things lying on the road well ahead of you.

A lot of motorists do not bother to dip their headlights on motorways, presumably thinking that the roads are so wide that nobody will be dazzled. The fact that they themselves may be dazzled by other drivers should show them that this is untrue, yet they still go on with headlights blazing away.

Eventually motorways will all have some sort of barrier to eliminate dazzle and prevent cars crashing across the middle, but until that day comes drivers should dip their lights as on any other road.

Remember, however, that dipped headlights reduce your range of vision, and you must always drive by what you can see. The braking distance for 70 m.p.h. is 245 feet and the thinking distance is 70 feet, making a total of 315 feet, or 105 yards. Can you see that far on dipped headlights? Obviously not, and I hope by now it is unnecessary for me to point out what you have to do about it.

Leaving the Motorway

Leaving the motorway should be simple, but again there are dangers, and I often see drivers making strange mistakes. You must know the point at which you want to leave, and you should know the exit number as well as the name of the town you require. If you know the exit number you can tell yourself in advance that it is the next but two, then the next but one, and now . . . this one.

There will be one signpost a mile from the exit and another half a mile from it, and then markings at 300 yards, 200 yards and 100 yards. You should be in the nearside lane by the time you reach the 300 yards mark. Then you cross into the deceleration lane and reduce speed. Use your speedometer when you do this, because it is easy to misjudge speed after a period of motorway driving. Be extra careful about speed for a few minutes after leaving the motorway, for the same reason.

Learners

Some of my hints for motorway driving may seem old and simple to many drivers, but that is inevitable. In Britain there is no system for teaching the everyday motorist how to behave on motorways, which is unfortunate. L drivers are banned, so a learner cannot be taken on motorways before his test. He is not allowed on the motorway during his test, and it is unlikely that he will ask for special instruction afterwards. All of this is most unfortunate because, as I said at the beginning of the chapter, motorways are safe, but some of the drivers on them are not. If the drivers are to be made safe too they must be taught.

I cannot see any reason why a learner considered ready for his test should not be taken to a motorway with a Ministry of Transport Approved Instructor, and I cannot see why examiners should not have discretion to take drivers there if they appear good enough. It seems wrong that a man who is just a few minutes away from being able to take his wife and children up and down every road in the country should not learn something about the roads that are becoming the major driving network.

Everything that makes roads safer should be part of our motoring lives.

15

Night Driving

Some people hate night driving; others love it. Usually the haters are nervous in cars at night, probably because they do not appreciate either the good things or the bad things about driving in the dark. Often the people who love it are over-confident, and that can be just as bad as being nervous.

I neither love it nor hate it. I enjoy all forms of driving, but I do like to try to make everything as simple and safe as possible, and night driving has complications which may interfere with simplicity and safety. I enjoy the snug feeling of driving a car on a cold, wet night with the sound of rain on the roof and the wipers working away, but I do not enjoy the strain of watching the dark road ahead made even darker by the fact that the lights have to penetrate rain as well as night. I enjoy knowing that the roads are more clear, but I do not enjoy meeting streams of cars with badly adjusted headlights throwing too much light in my direction. I enjoy the solitude of a long night drive, but I do not enjoy the extra fatigue created by ensuring that I am driving safely through the darkness.

Your Headlights

Visibility, as ever, is one of the most important things, and at night you have to ensure that you can see and be seen. If your lights are going to dazzle the other drivers you are not satisfying the conditions, because the dazzled driver will not be able to see you clearly. Also, if your lights are so adjusted that they dazzle others while dipped you will not be getting full benefit from them on full beam, so you will not see as clearly as you should.

It is estimated that about half the cars in Britain have wrongly adjusted headlights. Adjustment should be checked every 5,000 miles or so, and the best checks are made at reputable garages. If your lights do not dip sufficiently, then they must also be aimed high when on full beam, so they will be tree-spotting instead of illuminating the farthest possible point of the road. Your visibility, and therefore your driving, will suffer.

I have known people complain about poor headlights when the only trouble has been bad adjustment. Some have actually added expensive spotlights instead of having a garage see to the headlights. Then they have gone off driving with lights that do not dip properly and a spotlight which does not dip at all and is never turned off. Sometimes they drive on the spotlight alone, which is a bad habit, as you cannot see the road ahead clearly with nothing but a long pencil beam, and looking along such a beam is more tiring to the eyes than driving on ordinary headlights properly adjusted.

It is most important that you should not dazzle other drivers at night, because they will not be able to see you clearly or may go off course towards you, or one may lose his temper and use his lights to dazzle you, creating a dangerous, pointless duel. Both of you may end the duel in evil tempers and drive on in nasty moods that will make one of you do something stupid enough to cause an accident.

At holiday time when the boot is fully loaded you should have your lights specially adjusted. The weight in the boot will alter the horizontal angle of the car, and the lights will point higher than usual.

Going Foreign

If you intend holidaying abroad with your car you must fit continental lights. I do not consider it sufficient just to put in bulbs that dip to the right. Continental headlights have a beam shaped differently from the beam of British lights, and you can buy bulbs or lighting units which dip to the right and give this sort of beam. Drivers abroad find the British type of beam more dazzling, perhaps because they are not accustomed to it, and they are very quick to use all their lights to blind you if you upset them.

The question whether you use white or amber lights abroad must be your own personal decision, and I think it is more important to have the correct shape of beam than to change the colour of your lights.

Many people believe in amber lights, even in Britain, because they consider that they give less risk of dazzle and that they penetrate fog better. The truth is that they do dazzle less but do not penetrate fog better than white lights, and the reason for both is the same. An amber light is less efficient than a white light of the same wattage, and it does not dazzle so much because it does not do anything so much. You simply do not see so well with an amber light.

Rear Vision

I like reversing lights. Every car should have one, but be careful to study the legal requirements if you plan to fit one yourself, because there are laws about lights. If you have no reversing lights or if the one on your car is not working, you can see reasonably by using the brake lights frequently, but an even better idea is to put on your trafficator, as this will not only give you frequent flashes to illuminate the rear of the car, but will warn other drivers and unseen pedestrians that you are engaged in some kind of manoeuvre.

You should not have any bright lights on inside the car while driving at night, as they will either distract you or interfere with your forward vision, or both. I like to use the rheostat on dash lights, so that I can have them dimmed for the open road and brighter in town. Bright lights on the dashboard out of town may reflect in the windscreen and become an irritation.

An illuminated magnifying glass is a useful aid to keep in the car if you do much night driving in strange areas, because eyes strained over a map in dim light will not be so willing to work properly when you start driving again.

Switch on Early

In Britain the official lighting-up time is rather meaningless, as it is usually pitch dark by then, and only incredibly stupid people would leave their lights off so late if driving. But many do leave it far too long before turning on some lights. They seem to think that driving in gathering dusk without lights proves them to be more clever than anyone else, while in truth it suggests that they are fools.

The sort of people who deliberately delay switching on lights do so because they claim to be able to see quite well enough, and they may even remark on their good night vision. The real question in early and middle dusk, however, is: Can other road-users see you?

Dark cars, especially black and grey ones, can be extremely difficult to see on a dark road with the heavy shadows of dusk if they do not have sidelights and rear lights showing. White cars, of course, are more visible in the evening, unless there is some mist or fog around, when they become invisible.

I always turn on my sidelights the moment I think someone

might have difficulty in seeing me, or when I think I could read my instruments better if lighted, or when I see another car with his lights on, whichever comes first. Naturally this means that in wooded country my lights go on earlier than they would elsewhere because of the dark shadows.

I start using my headlights the moment I think they would help me to see the road more clearly.

Dazzle

I believe in dipping my lights early if the road is straight, because one can experience dazzle from a car quite a long way off, and cars travelling quickly towards one another close at a remarkable speed. On a left-hand bend I dip early too if there is a car coming the other way, because on that sort of bend my lights would hit him long before his reached me. On a right-hand bend I usually do not dip so early, as the lights are pointing away from oncoming traffic, but on certain right-handers I find it an advantage to have my lights dipped to show up the verge more clearly.

I am always mindful of dazzle and keep my windscreen clean inside and out, because spots or smearing on a windscreen aggravate the dazzle problem for the driver. I am equally careful about not dazzling other drivers, including those behind me, so in towns I do not sit at traffic lights with my footbrake on and brake lights shining. If I am making a turn at lights I wait with my trafficator on until a car has stopped behind me, then I turn off until the lights change. This way the driver behind knows what I am going to do, and when I turn the trafficator on again it reminds him and warns cars coming the other way.

Dazzle from behind is irritating, and is caused either by a car following with undipped lights or badly adjusted lights, or else by running up too close. Dazzle from behind comes, of

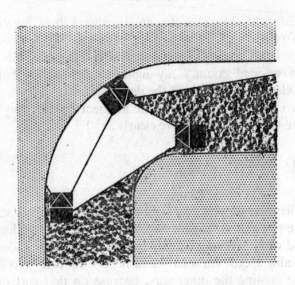

12. This diagram indicates headlight beam patterns on a bend. The car which is going left would dazzle both the other drivers if his lights remained undipped, but would not be dazzled by undipped lights from either of the other two cars. Therefore drivers going round a left-hand bend must take special care to dip early, but drivers going round a right-hand bend may not have to dip at all.

course, from your mirrors. If they are adjusted correctly you can see behind without moving your head, but this means that they reflect light from behind directly into your eyes.

Interior mirrors which dip are good, and on my own car I have one that dips automatically. It has a small photo-electric cell—like a photographic exposure meter—and this dips the mirror when light strikes it, and undips when there is no light. This is a nice device, but I am not so keen on the ones which dip your own headlights for you. This gadget has a photo-electric cell pointing forward, and when light from an oncoming car strikes the cell your headlights are dipped. Unfortunately they may also be dipped by reflected light from a window or a white house or a white-walled bridge, and that can be uncomfortable if it happens unexpectedly at a tricky corner. Apart from this, I prefer to have complete charge of my dipper.

There is a foolish practice, now illegal, of driving at night on an open road with sidelights only when following another car with his headlights on. You may not be following in his tracks exactly, and there could be something at the edge of the road which he missed because he could see it, and which you will hit because you cannot see it.

Night driving is one of the more important features of police training, and we used to take students out for long drives and give demonstration night drives. This cannot be done with a book, but I think reprinting an actual commentary is as near as one can get to it. I have tape-recorded a night-driving commentary, and this time I used a car with automatic transmission, and I mention one or two points about driving such cars which I hope will be useful.

Tape Recording

Here is the commentary:

'I am driving along a fairly quiet suburban road and it is dusk. The brake lights and indicator lights are beginning to be a bit bright. Some cars have their lights on already and I have mine on too. I am coming towards a T-junction and I am turning left. Mirror. Signal. There is nothing behind me at the moment, but there is somebody in front and he may want to know where I am going. Looking to the right, and there are several vehicles coming.

'I am driving a three-and-a-half litre automatic, so the question of gears does not arise. I am in D2. I can come out now, into a four-lane dual carriageway. It is getting dark rapidly. The car has just changed into top. There is one car a long way behind and one in front turning right. I am already in the nearside lane. Speed is just over 30. The car behind is signalling that he is going right. I'll flash my lights down the inside to let the car ahead know I'm coming through.

'There is a pedestrian crossing; it's clear. Mirror. Nothing behind. The road ahead is clear for quite a long way. It is well lit—sodium lighting, with the lights fairly close together. Almost like daylight. No need for dipped headlights here. There's a turning on the left and one car waiting to come out. There's a roundabout ahead and I'm going right. Mirror. There's one chap behind coming up quite quickly, but he's still a long way off. Signal that I'm moving to the offside lane, and cancel signal now. I'm looking to the right at the round-about and I can go straight away. Keeping to the right-hand lane, and now I'm opposite the last turning on the left and I signal that I'm going out at the next exit. Pedestrian crossing at the exit is clear.

'There's a bit more traffic now and the road surface has changed, but it is still very good indeed. The lighting has changed too. It is white, but still good. Can see far more clearly. It is quite dark now overhead.

'The traffic lights ahead are red, and I'm going straight on, so I take the left-hand lane in case one of the cars waiting on the offside decides to give a late right-turn signal. The one in front of me is turning left and he has his trafficator going, and it is going on and on and on and on and it's blinding. Lights are changing to green. Moving off.

'I'm going uphill now, several vehicles behind keeping a good distance, nothing ahead. Surface is good and lighting is good.

'There is another set of traffic lights about a quarter of a mile ahead and I am going right. Signal now. Now I am in the offside lane and braking gently. I still leave the car in drive. Stopping for the lights now. The driver in the nearside lane is out washing his windscreen. Nobody behind me. I will leave my signal on, keep an eye on the mirror so that if somebody does come up behind me I can turn it off.

'The lights have changed now and there is nobody coming

towards me, so I can go. Still in a good, wide road, different surface but still good and well lit. There are driveways to the houses on the left, which I am watching.

'There's a learner backing out of one. He has seen me and, instead of waiting, he's turned his wheel more sharply so that he's on the pavement. I'm giving him plenty of room. I think I need to.

'The road widens now. It's very wide indeed and there are parked vehicles on the left, but no drivers. There is a school sign, but at this time there will be no children. There are no lights in the school, so there are no evening classes there. Now it is dual-carriageway and 40 m.p.h. sign, so I'll push the speed up a little. There's one car ahead turning right, two cars a bit too close behind. The road turns to the left, a long bend. No problem. Now the one behind is overtaking, and I'm doing a good 40. He has passed now. There's a slow-moving lorry ahead. Mirror. There's a gap, so I can move out. Signal and I'm moving out. Cancel signal.

'I'm catching up with the lorry. He is very steady, so there's no need for a warning. I'm passing the lorry now and there's a car behind about three feet off my tail. I am doing 40. Now I can move in to the left. I am doing 43 and the car behind is going past quite rapidly.

'The dual-carriageway ends now, but the road is still quite wide, double white line in the middle. There is a slight rise with two lanes up and one down. The speed limit has gone up to 50, so I can go a little faster.

'Now we are on the brow of the hill and traffic lights ahead are red. There are some cars in the nearside lane, nothing in my lane, and there is a right-turn lane on my offside. Braking and stopping and I'll put the handbrake on. The brake lights on this car are very bright and I don't want to blind whoever comes behind. The lights are changing and I can go.

'The street lighting ends soon, on headlights. Make sure they are dipped. There's quite a lot of traffic ahead, so I'll position myself where the dipped lights will strike on the ground, not on the back of the car ahead. There is a roundabout and I will be going left.

'The roundabout is well lit; braking for it now. I'll turn my headlights off because I'm closing on the chap in front as I brake. I'll signal left. The roundabout is clear, so I'm turning left now.

'This is a very narrow road and the road surface has changed three times in as many yards. It is badly lit. I am on dipped headlights again. There are bright spots and dark patches where nothing would show without headlights. Nothing ahead and nothing behind. The road widens a bit now and the lighting improves a little. There's a small shopping area and a fish-and-chip shop. It's not too late for kids, so I'll watch for them near the fish shop.

'I'm through the shopping area now, and the lighting finishes. The road runs sharply downhill and I can see ahead that there is a bend right.

'There is nothing coming towards me. I am fairly high, which helps me to see that there are no lights at all coming towards me. I'm braking now for the bend and I will move the gear lever into hold, which drops the car into second gear. Now going smoothly through the corner, and there are still no lights coming towards me.

'My lights are undipped and across the hedges I can see some rear lights. Move lever back to drive. There are some bends, all of them easy. Now the road straightens and I dip my lights. I'm closing on the car whose tail lights I saw across the hedges. The road bears left, still narrow, and I am now at a following distance to the car in front so that my dipped lights will not dazzle him. Now the road goes right and I have a magnificent view ahead. Nothing coming. Mirror. I can overtake. Quick flash of my lights to let him know I'm coming, and I can go through. No lights coming towards me, so back to full headlights.

'The road goes left now, quite sharply, and I will keep out as far as I can in case there are any pedestrians, and I am braking a little. All is clear and I am rounding the bend now.

'The road straightens and widens a little. Mirror. There are lights behind, still round the bend. They're moving very fast, very fast indeed. Now the lights are round the bend and he's coming up very fast behind me. He's flashing his lights at me. I'll hold a steady pace, in fact, I'll ease the accelerator a little to let him get through faster. And now he goes past.

'There's a right-hand bend ahead, quite an easy one. We're round it and there are lights coming towards me. I am dipping. The other lights are still on high beam, a bit dazzling. Now he's dipped. There are two other cars behind him. We're passing one another now, and the third car has very badly adjusted headlights.

'I'm not looking at them. I'm keeping my eyes well to my own side of the road to keep out of the dazzle and pick out what I can. I have eased my speed down.

'There is a T-junction ahead. Mirror. Nothing. I am going to the left, so I am moving well into the left and signalling for traffic going across the junction. Just two cars coming, so I stay in drive. Now I can go and I accelerate away. This road is de-restricted which nowadays means 70 m.p.h. The road snakes around, so I will not try to do 70. I am doing 55.

'Now it straightens and I can increase my speed and there is a fork ahead.

'I am slowing down for the fork, going right. There are a lot of trees, and if there was anybody on sidelights alone I would not see him. It is all clear, so I accelerate again.

'There is a T-junction now and I will be going right. Mirror. Nobody behind. Slowing right down, but the main road is clear too, so I can get out, now. I am on the main road now and accelerating. There is a pub on the left with a large forecourt and some movement, so I am leaving plenty of room to the left.

'There is a lorry ahead running slowly on dipped lights. He undips and dips them again to signal that all is clear. I acknowledge. I can see it is for myself so I overtake—mirror, move out, accelerate.

'The road narrows and there's another lorry about a quarter of a mile ahead. Traffic coming the other way, all dipped and lights badly adjusted except for the second one. Now I am waiting behind the lorry for the road to clear.

'Now the traffic has gone and I can ease out a little to take a good look ahead. The lorry is on dipped lights. There appears to be a bend—yes, there is a bend.

'Going round the bend now, and the road is straight and my lights are on full beam and the road ahead is clear. I accelerate up to 70 m.p.h.'

16

---•◆•---

Fast Driving

Speed is a much misunderstood thing. Some people regard it as evil and frightening, to others it is a luxury, to others a way of life. In fact, it is just part of a car's equipment, a built-in essential which should be thought of as a physical thing which can be used or misused. It is rather like an axe. It can be a killer, or it can do useful work. It can damage the user, or it may protect him from danger; it can maim the innocent, it can disfigure the careless. In the wrong hands or used the wrong way, it can be a lethal, offensive weapon. If blunted it is inefficient.

Once you learn to think of speed like a tool you get the whole matter in perspective. A tradesman who has served an apprenticeship can use his tools carefully and safely and well, but the enthusiastic do-it-yourself addict who does not practise and think will not get the same results as the tradesman, and will not be so safe when using the tool. There are gifted people with a natural bent for do-it-yourself, and they seem to succeed and be safe by instinct, without a lot of training or practice. There are the same sort of people among drivers, and they are just as rare—so rare in fact, that it would be foolish to assume that you are one of them, even if you are.

Flowing Along

Speed is just part of fast driving, but if you are to drive fast safely you must be able to use and control it. It should not be wasted. A forester chopping down a tree will place every stroke of the axe precisely to give most effective cutting, and he will not waste effort or blunt the axe too quickly by too many strokes. A careless amateur will take three times as long, use twice as many strokes and expend four times as much energy. The forester will work with a flowing series of movements, each blending with the other, and there will be rhythm. The amateur will work jerkily, without flow and with as much rhythm as a temperamental pneumatic drill.

Driving is the same. The secret of good, fast driving is flow and rhythm. Any other sort of driving is wasteful, uses too much petrol and energy, and will be slower in the end.

Misusing Speed

A typical misuse of speed occurs on roads with lots of traffic lights. The bad driver rushes away as fast as he can accelerate and then has to brake to a standstill at the next lights. The good driver does not accelerate so harshly and judges his distances so that he may still be rolling when he reaches the next lights and may, in fact, be able to go straight across them without stopping, thus getting ahead of the bad driver.

In that situation the bad driver has been wasteful in three ways. He wasted petrol by his fierce acceleration and he wasted it again when he braked. It is not generally appreciated that braking wastes petrol, but it does because the only way to replace the speed you have lost is to accelerate again. In this case the third wastage referred to is driver-energy, and that driver will tire more quickly than the better, smoother man.

Slow Down to go Fast

Jerky driving is bad driving because it shows that the driver does not plan. And if you want to drive fast you must plan, plan, plan all the time.

If you have ambitions to be a fast driver I would suggest that your first step would be to slow down by at least ten miles an hour when you are out of town.

Now practise giving a commentary on your driving. Comment on what you see *and what you are going to do about it.* If you have difficulty in mentioning all you see ask yourself whether you are going too fast.

To know the features of the system of car-control is not enough; one must time one's approach to a hazard properly.

When you reach that point on the approach where you consider using the horn, see if you are in a position where a horn note would do some good by warning others of your approach *before* they can see you.

If your hand goes to the horn button when you could be seen by the man in the side road, you are starting the sequence of control far too late.

If you are remarking on things as you pass, then stop commenting and start again as far ahead as possible.

Raise your eyes to a point farther down the road than your normal place of focus. Then eliminate all hard, sudden foot pressures on brake and accelerator by intelligent anticipation.

Concentrate on doing these things for a few thousand miles, and if you have really worked at it you should find that you are now completing journeys quicker than before, even though you may not reach the top speeds that you reached before. You will have developed flow, you will have learned how to plan, you will have become a better driver.

Once you have achieved this you can start building up your speeds again, but gently, so that you do not undo the good you have done.

Apart from the safety bonus of improved car-control, and the financial bonus from more economical use of petrol and mechanical parts, there is another benefit. You will not get tired so quickly, and on a long journey this will mean fewer stops for cups of tea, and that will make a big difference to your average speed.

Fatigue

The question of fatigue is very important for fast driving, and even for slow driving. It can be caused by tension or by strain, or by noise or by discomfort as well as the obvious thing of just getting tired. A driver should be relaxed and comfortable, and this requires a good seat as well as a good seating position.

A lot of today's cars do not have good seats, and I have heard of people who have ever gone to the expense of changing cars because of getting pains in the back from the driving seat of a car they otherwise liked. This sort of thing is a needless waste of money. If your seat is not comfortable you can buy a new one and have it fitted, although most of the seats bought in this way are so specialist that they look odd in an ordinary car.

I think noisy cars should be made quieter, and the motoring magazines carry advertisements from firms which sell quietening kits that are easily fitted.

Both these improvements should make the time you take for journeys seem shorter, but you must also have the car in good mechanical order. Why chop a tree with a blunt axe when it can be sharpened? Why try to drive quickly in a car that is out of tune, when a few pounds spent wisely will improve performance and reduce petrol consumption?

I am not suggesting that you should go out and buy a host of bolt-on goodies, but I do think that every car should be taken periodically to one of the places with special equipment for checking carburation and valve-timing and ignition settings. In most cases you will come away feeling that you are driving a new car.

The only other piece of advice I think I can give to prospective fast drivers is: Read my book again, and good luck.

But don't trust to luck. Try tolerance, patience, concentration and common sense.

There is nothing I enjoy more than driving quickly, but I never forget that there is another day tomorrow.

Index

BOOKS FOR YOUR JOURNEYS

On Tour

A book of unusual interest for the motorist: 5000 miles through England, Wales and Scotland in search of

THE REALMS OF ARTHUR

An Illustrated Journey
through the Arthurian Legend

by Helen Hill Miller. Over 150 illustrations and 7 maps: 60s

Good Camping Cookery

GOURMET IN THE GALLEY

Complete Guide to Practical Holiday Cookery

600 easily prepared recipes – varied, imaginative and stimulating dishes that make holiday cooking and eating a real pleasure.

by Felice Martel Morrison.   (Waterproof binding):   30s

For Relaxation

HOW NOT TO LOSE AT POKER

Indispensable for players of poker and poker dice – an answer in simple terms to all possible betting problems up to completion of the hand.

by Jeffery Lloyd Castle.   30s